RACE TO FAME
THE INSIDE STORY OF THE
BLUENOSE

"Be our strength in hours of weakness,
In our wanderings be our guide;
Through endeavours, failure, danger,
Saviour be thou at our side."
                    Maria Willis, 1864

(The Book of Common Praise, Hymn 454)

RACE TO FAME
THE INSIDE STORY OF THE
BLUENOSE

Captain C.K. Darrach, M.B.E.

LANCELOT PRESS
Hantsport, Nova Scotia

ISBN 0-88999-280-0

Published 1985

LANCELOT PRESS LIMITED, Hantsport, N.S.

Office and plant situated on Highway No. 1, ½ mile east of Hantsport.

To Schooner *Bluenose*!
  A fascinating example of Nova Scotia skill and craftmanship!
  This book is dedicated to a glorious era graced by the reign of fast and able schooners.

To Schooner *Bluenose II*!
  A worthy daughter of a great mother!
A further remembrance of Nova Scotia skill and craftmanship, of courage and seamanship supreme!

INTRODUCTION

Very often over the past several years I have listened to remarks made by young and old alike, about the schooner *Bluenose*. From these remarks and queries I have come to the conclusion that a great majority forget, or do not know, the saga of our famous *Bluenose* — a Nova Scotia fishing schooner which, because of her fame, is portrayed on the Canadian ten-cent piece and whose memory is now honoured by her replica, *Bluenose II* — the Nova Scotia Department of Tourism's Ambassador of Good Will.

On the following pages I hope to present to readers a great heritage, worthy of recording, and to justly honour Senator Wm. Dennis, then the owner of the *Halifax Herald* and the *Halifax Chronicle*, who created the idea for an International Fishing Schooner Race by donating the Halifax Herald Trophy. This trophy was given to the winner of the fastest schooner racing in the Nova Scotia and New England fishing fleets.

Credit should be given to many who helped *Bluenose* attain her fame. Mr. H.R. Silver, Chairman of the Sailing Committee and his committee members are to be noted. The designers, builders, sailmakers and riggers, and the twenty-two other schooners in the races with their five hundred fishing captains and crew members, deserve worthy mention. Of course, much recognition must be given to Captain Angus Walters who "steered" *Bluenose* through the races to win the trophy and "Queen of the Atlantic" title.

As a crewman from the beginning in October, 1920 to the finale in October, 1938, I fondly think of that time as a "dramatic challenge" and I am grateful to the management of Lancelot Press of Hantsport, N.S., for their cover design and the publication of this manuscript.

C. Darrach

CONTENTS

ACKNOWLEDGEMENTS

Fishing schooner captains kept a journal-type log in which entries would be written at the end of the day. Anything unusual or different from the normal routine would be written down at the time of happening. The incident would be described in detail in case the information should be required at a later date. However, this was not the log book-type kept from minute to minute by the Officer of the Watch onboard merchant vessels.

Accordingly, I must thank my own diary and notes which were written at the end of the day. Some abstracts were taken from the skipper's log, the Shipping Master's records and newspaper clippings, for dates, times and names. Particularly, I wish to thank Mr. Paul Wentzell, the Shipping Master at the port of Lunenburg.

I am indebted to the Canadian publication *The Schooner Bluenose* by A.D. Merkel, and the American publication *Fast and Able* by Gordon Thomas. From these publications I was able to confirm some of the entries in my notes.

To the Ven. H.B. Wainwright I owe special thanks. He read my manuscript and had the courage and personality to suggest there was need of revision. I am grateful for his concern and time in editing the manuscript.

Mr. Gordon Sinclair kindly gave his permission for me to say that he was with the *Toronto Star* and that he made the trip from Lunenburg to Gloucester aboard *Bluenose*, for the 1938 series. He was covering the story of the races.

Mr. J. Frank Willis and Captain W.E.S. Briggs also made the voyage on behalf of C.B.C. Radio. Both these gentlemen 'crossed the bar' some time ago.

Mr. G.W. Dennis, of The Halifax Herald Limited, very kindly gave his permission for me to reprint "The Conditions of Deed of Gift, *The Halifax Herald*'s North Atlantic Fishermen's Trophy".

FOREWORD

When speaking of the International Fishermen's Schooner Races, 1920-1938, between Atlantic Canadian Maritime deep sea fishing schooners and their counterparts from the New England States, I suggest we see the competition as a challenge rather than a professional sporting event, simply because of its origin. The personnel involved were, of course, professional in every respect. The schooners were of the highest standard of design, construction and specification. The event, itself, was unique, and it is safe to say that no other seagoing contest has ever attracted greater interest. Nor has any one sailing vessel achieved greater renown than the Lunenburg, Nova Scotia, Grand Bank schooner *Bluenose*, with her famous Captain Angus Walters. Together they became legendary and, to this day, continue as such in the archives of Canadian Maritime history.

Bluenose dimensions.

Overall length	143'
Water-line length	112'
Beam	27'
Draft	15'10"
Depth at main hatch	11'6"
Height: deck to head of main topmast	125'10"
Height: deck to head of fore-topmast	108'6"
Mainboom	81'

Bluenose, like all ships, was a calculated creation in volume, coefficient, stability and sail plan, and she was perfect in every sequence. For 18 years, Captain Angus Walters was in command. Captain Angus and *Bluenose* were never outclassed or beaten. Together, they retired as champions.

Bluenose was the 121st schooner to be launched from Smith and Rhuland shipyards of Lunenburg. Her construction, based on skill and experience, was of high standard. Her design was slightly different to the previous conventional schooners. Men who worked on her building were said to have remarked:

"She was a fine vessel but different to the others in the fleet."

Some schooners, carrying all sail under strong wind force, will bury and drag water. Too much green water will tumble on deck. The excess weight causes awkward and difficult performance. Other schooners will heel to a degree where the equilibrium is unstable.

Bluenose tended to heave out, but shipped no water on deck and maintained a stable equilibrium at all times. When she was under full sail and the gusts of wind had a force of 35 m.p.h. coming in from forward of the beam, with sheets trimmed she would show a high windward side, while the lee side maintained a stable center of buoyancy, enabling her to cope with and benefit from the wind force. Under these conditions, she would show safe stability and good response to the rudder angle. When required, very few schooners are capable of that sort of performance. Hove to, under foresail only, in gale force conditions, she would range ahead and maintain a windward position. I believe this explains what the experienced shipwrights were talking about when they referred to her as 'different.' They recognized something new in the under water profile.

Operating out on the fishing banks, the crews averaged 20 men (two to a dory, eight dories plus header, throater, cook and captain).

When engaged in international race events, the crew averaged 28 to 30 men. Considering the fact that the fishing fleets in the ports of Lunenburg and LaHave had more than 50 schooners, it was not difficult to find enough skilled able seamen to make up a race crew. When fully rigged, a schooner has approximately 29 halyards, with sheets and downhauls secured to belaying pins. Each one has its own place and purpose. A crew member must know them by name and also know where to find them. A crew member must also be ready to go aloft when required. These rules were not laid down but they were understood as necessary qualifications.

Several captains of other schooners temporarily forsook the dignity of rank for the dramatic thrill of being crew members onboard a racing schooner. It was not unusual that a highline fishing captain be observed wearing a cook's cap and apron and carrying out the forecastle cooking duties for the event. 'Pride' and 'dignity', as these men saw it, were earned by 'skill' and 'versatility'. They were competent men in the many phases of a seaman's profession. Many of them held certificates which were the result of academic study and Board of Trade examination.

To what extent Captain Angus Walters personally realized the outstanding qualities he possessed in the art of sailing large schooners is unknown. He acted modestly but there was the power of command in his orders and 'suggestions'. His colleagues, the captains and the dory men, held great respect for his judgement and seamanship. He was never openly critical of the way in which other people operated. Any opinion he had of them was kept to himself. However, I do know that though he had admiration for the design and construction of the rival American schooners, he also seemed to believe they had too much sail area.

Captain Angus Walters was a dedicated master in the art of sailing large fore and aft rigged fishing schooners. He had the instinct and knowledge how to balance and co-ordinate the components that forced a schooner hull through the ocean in any kind of sea. Once he had examined the coefficient of a hull, he understood the order in which ballast trim, sail plan and helm control must be arranged. When his hand was on the wheel, he could feel the ship's impulse and would act upon it. He had a natural aptitude to recognize any unco-ordinated situation and how to correct it. He showed this flair long before he commanded *Bluenose*.

Previously, he had been in command of the schooner *Gilbert Walters*, which was a large, lofty, full coefficient knockabout, with little in appearance to indicate a fast sailer. It did not take Angus long to discover her qualities. He gave proof of this on 11 October 1920, during the elimination race. On that day, *Gilbert Walters* was trailing behind eight fast vessels, but came up and passed them all. She had a substantial lead when her fore-topmast broke. By the time the loose rigging and broken mast had been cleared away, *Delawana* passed *Gilbert Walters* and won the race.

Nova Scotians built, at least, six new deep sea fishing schooners with the emphasis on fast sailing qualities. Some turned out better than others. They were *Bluenose, Haligonian, Canadia, Keno, Mahaska* and *Mayotte*. The first three were rated in that order. *Mahaska* was not up to it. *Keno* and *Mayotte* were short lived and had little or no opportunity to be tested.

The New England States built seven beautiful looking schooners, of which *Columbia* and *Mayflower* were, undoubtedly, the fastest.

It was fatal to make a mistake or have a 'misfortune' aboard *Bluenose* when competing with *Columbia*. *Mayflower* was disqualified and never did compete, but she was very good and a fast vessel. Regardless, *Bluenose* continued to be the fastest and most able, schooner. After 18 years and twelve potential challengers, she remained the champion sailer of the North Atlantic fishing schooners, 1921-1938.

The last series, off Gloucester and Boston, might well be considered a glorious finale to the Grand Bankers from Cape Cod, U.S.A. to Cape Bauld, Newfoundland. *Bluenose* beat *Gertrude L. Thebaud* to win that series, 26 October 1938, off Cape Ann, by two minutes and 50 seconds.

Gertrude L. Thebaud returned to her berth in Gloucester. *Bluenose* returned to Lunenburg. Both schooners were stripped of topmasts and mainbooms. Sail were reduced to 'jumbo', 'foresail' and 'stormsail'. Diesel engines were installed. There were no others of the conventional sailing fleets to be found. It was the end of an era. The 'topsail schooners of the Grand Bank fleets' had disappeared.

The foreword would not be complete without mention

being made of the humourous and often satirical discussions of the forecastle gang aboard these large schooners. Forecastle accommodations included sleeping bunks for 20 men. There was also a spacious gallery complex, and a table to seat twelve persons for meals. In addition, there was enough space for each man to have a sea chest locker. The food, by tradition and demand, was excellent. While races were on, these 'rugged', 'healthy', 'competent' characters were relaxed, much more so than when engaged in actual fishing operations. Despite the mixture of captains and dorymen, there was no class distinction. By forecastle tradition, they 'ridiculed the old man' (captain), 'teased the cook' and talked seriously of weather conditions. Often they talked about the acres and acres of salt cod which were spread out to sun-dry on flakes along the Lunenburg County coast line. (This concerned the fish they had caught earlier in the year and which yet had to be sun-dried and marketed.)

If the 'old man' was in the least aware of the remarks made about him, he paid no attention because he, too, had occupied a forecastle bunk, before he had worked his way up to the status of captain.

He understood all this was taking place while tied alongside the wharf. There was no radio or T.V. He also knew that, when under way, it was a different story. All hands, then, would be alert with strained eyes and serious concentration, focussed on clouds, wind and sea state and, of course, on the manoeuvers of the rival schooner.

With the knowledge that the Grand Banker has vanished and not likely ever to return, it is my hope and endeavour that some authentic information will continue to be available for future generations to read and appreciate. It is also my hope that those who visit the Canadian Sports Hall of Fame, in Toronto, may appreciate, in greater measure, the memory of Angus Walters and the schooner *Bluenose*. May they link these names as reminders of, at least, two centuries of maritime craftsmanship, seamanship and sound economic industry.

I had the opportunity to be part if it in different ways. Soon after the turn of the century, instead of continuing in the schoolroom, I was in the forecastle. My career was of my own choosing. At times, it was rugged but, all in all, it was good.

Chapter 1

Through the years, a system had developed for the financing of fishing schooners. All those Lunenburg vessels that fished on the Grand Bank of Newfoundland, Greenland, Labrador and the southerly sections of the Canadian continental shelf were financed in the same way and *Bluenose* was no exception.

If a man, from his youth up, had gained a good reputation as a potential fishing skipper while serving as a doryman onboard any of the fleet of 50 or more schooners, and he had the ambition, and his potential was recognized by the skippers he had served under, it was likely he could raise the money to command a schooner of his own.

He would make known his intention by canvassing the community, offering the opportunity to invest by taking a one sixty-fourth share. There was no such thing as a subsidy and seldom ever a loan. Fish merchants, ship chandlers, sailmakers, blacksmiths and the actual fishermen, financed from their savings and earnings, would form the bulk of the investors. The total cost of a vessel was divided by 64 to determine the cost of a one-share investment, and was referred to as a 'sixty-fourth'.

Captain Thomas Himmelman and Captain Angus Walters had, long since, progressed through that stage and, by 1919, were rated among the highline skippers bringing home good paying catches in the schooners *Delawana* and *Gilbert*

Walters. These were the two skippers whose vessels placed first and second in an elimination race to choose the challenger to race against the best schooner from the Gloucester, Mass. fleet. There would be an International Fishermen's Schooner Race for a trophy and a purse.

Fishing schooners racing! Why? What was this all about? Well! If you had been a sports enthusiast and had been keeping up to date in world events, you would have known that the outstanding yachting event of 1920 was to take place off Sandy Hook, New York. There was little radio, and certainly no television, to publicize the coming race, but the city and town daily newspapers were full of it, and other people were kept informed by the weekly papers.

The British yacht *Shamrock IV* had challenged the American defender *Resolute*, with the hope that *Shamrock* would win and return to the United Kingdom with the America Cup. The America Cup is the 100 Guineas Cup won by the United States yacht *America*, in a race around the Isle of Wight in 1851.

The *America* may have been, or may not have been, the faster sailer in that race. There is no doubt she was the first to finish, but it is reported that her shallow draught enabled her to choose a shorter overall distance to round the Isle. However, *America* was named the winner and brought the cup home to the United States. In the future, the cup would be known as the America Cup.

There were many challengers in the succeeding years, but none of them were successful in taking the cup back to Great Britain and, often, the races were marred by disputes.

This time, the race was to be between *Resolute* and *Shamrock IV*. *Resolute* was, I believe, sailing out of the N.Y.Y.C., while *Shamrock IV*, of the Royal Ulster Yacht Club (R.U.Y.C.) was owned by Sir Thomas Lipton.

As the fishing schooners of Gloucester and Lunenburg arrived home from the Grand Bank they learned that the U.S. *Resolute* was, once again, the winner. They also heard that the race had been postponed one fine July morning because there had been a 23 knot breeze. Such news echoed and re-echoed among schooner fishermen from Newfoundland to Gloucester. Men who lived by wind and sail were not pleased. They believed they could put on a show which would be an exhibition of sail-carrying. The controversy, in the forecastles, on street corners and in the bars, became so intense that, finally, Senator W.H. Dennis, proprietor of the newspaper, *Halifax Herald*, was able to announce an elimination race would be held off Halifax in October, for an international trophy to be called the Halifax Herald Trophy. There would also be a cash prize of $3,000.00.

It is doubtful the senator could foresee that the last race for the Trophy, 26 October 1938, would mark the end of the era of Grand Bank fishing schooners.

In the days before the advent of highrise buildings, the greater part of Halifax Harbour could be seen from the eastern and southern slopes of Citadel Hill. Also, the broad Atlantic could be seen extending to the horizon, where shipping joined the trade route to Europe.

People, crossing over Citadel Hill on the morning of 11 October 1920, watched the manoeuvers of nine, large, fast and able Lunenburg salt fishing schooners as they headed towards a starting line one mile south of George's Island.

They saw schooners of 140' overall length, with masts extending 120' above deck. Each vessel had a sail area spread of not less than 9000 square feet of cotton canvas sail. The sails were as white as freshly laundered sheets and were neatly trimmed over long black hulls. Rolls of clear white foam pushed out where the bow cut through the water.

On that morning, the atmosphere was clear with a cool 18 knot breeze. At that distance, the names of the schooners could not be seen with the naked eye, but those present were:

Schooner	Captain	Town
Delawana	Thomas Himmelman	Lunenburg
Gilbert Walters	Angus Walters	Lunenburg
Alcala	Roland Kinckle	Lunenburg
Independence	Albert Himmelman	Lunenburg
Mona Marie	Lemuel Ritchey	LaHave
Ruby L. Pentz	Calvin Lohnes	LaHave
Bernice Zinck	Daniel Zinck	Lunenburg
Democracy	William Deal	Lunenburg
Freda Himmelman	Alvin Himmelman	Lunenburg

Each schooner's name was printed on her bow. The course would take them six miles from the starting line to buoy #1, Inner Automatic, then on a triangular course of ten miles to Sambro Light Vessel, seven miles southeast to Automatic, six miles back to buoy #1, and six miles up the harbour to the start and finish line, a distance of 35 miles. The windward tacking would increase the distance to, roughly, 45 miles.

After the start of the race, the wind increased to fresh puffs of 25 knots. All day long, *Delawana*, *Gilbert Walters* and *Alcala* continued to threaten one another for first place. However, it seemed evident *Gilbert Walters* and *Delawana* were so evenly matched, tacking to windward, that the winner would be in doubt down to the very end, unless a mistake or misfortune occurred, and that is what happened. Five miles seaward of the finish line, *Gilbert Walters* broke her foretopmast, resulting in the loss of balloon and fore-topsail. Captain Angus Walters, her skipper, had the wheel and was keeping every square inch of canvas filled with wind and was driving for the finish line. At the same moment, Captain Thomas Himmelman was at the wheel of *Delawana*, less than a quarter of a mile from *Gilbert Walters*. Tommie had the same driving attitude and kept *Delawana's* lee rail awash. When he saw what had happened to *Gilbert Walters*, he realized *Delawana* now had the chance of winning. He was right.

Times at the finish line:

Delawana	5 hrs	07'	00"
Gilbert Walters	5	12	42
Alcala	5	16	00

By 5 hrs. 43'42" all nine schooners had crossed the finish line. Gratuitously, harbour tugboats pushed them alongside water-front jettys as the sails were being furled. The crews went below for the second warm meal of the day, at 1730. It was a good one. The other one had been breakfast at 0630. I shared in those meals. I was fortunate enough to be one of that crew. It was always good to be with a man like Tommie.

That night, skippers and crews were entertained at the Halifax and Queen hotels. It was a gracious reward for all our efforts. We had given up two weeks, at least, to rig, ballast and sail from LaHave and Lunenburg to Halifax. On our return, we would unrig and unballast. It was a true example of the seriousness of carrying sail and of our concern to excel in a sporting event.

In the meantime, in the port of Gloucester, Mass., fishermen were devoting the same time and energy in choosing a challenger to race against *Delawana*, Canada's defender of The Halifax Herald Trophy.

Their elimination race was run over the Cape Ann triangle, off Gloucester. The *Esperanto* won, with Captain Marty Welch at the wheel. He and his crew would sail *Esperanto* to Halifax for a series of first two out of three races over the same triangle which had seen *Delawana* win her race. The time limit was so fixed that less than a 20 knot breeze would be insufficient.

Just before this, *Esperanto* had arrived home from the Bank where she had spent most of the previous six months. However, when she sailed into Halifax Harbour, it looked as if the schooner had just been launched. In just a few days, her masts had been scraped down. She shone with tallow. Her cabin house, hatches and bulwark rails glistened white. Her long black sides were adorned with the conventional fore and aft yellow stripe, just above the freeing ports of the bulwark. This was a highlight to the black sides and it also graced the sheerline curve. "Yankee" style has a flair for this kind of thing. The hull and sail plans were smart and picturesque.

The match was over in two races, *Esperanto* being the winner. Marty and his crew set sail in her for the return to Gloucester, carrying with them the Halifax Herald Trophy and a $4,000.00 cash prize.

The times on Saturday, 29 October 1920, were:

Esperanto   5 hrs   59'   56"
Delawana   6 hrs   18'   48"

This win of *Esperanto* over *Delawana* brought about the building of *Bluenose* and, eventually, *Bluenose II*.

Even before *Esperanto* had left for her home port, the talk on the street corner and in the forecastle was tinged with dismay and the determination to bring back the Trophy to Nova Scotia. A schooner must be found. *Esperanto* had several sister schooners in the Gloucester fleet who were just as trim and, possibly, much faster than she. *Delawana* and *Gilbert Walters*, at that time, no doubt, were the fastest of the Lunenburg bankers. Therefore, a new vessel would have to be built.

I was not onboard *Delawana*, 29 October and 1 November. It was the fall mackerel season. I had a small interest in a little mackerel netter and I was also part of her crew. I could not afford the time ashore to go yachting. We had a 16 hour day of hard work. Racing was a much more relaxed routine. Once the vessel is under way with a good breeze, she is let drive for all she is worth, "and may the best boat win". Afterwards, there is the going ashore and mingling with the rival crews. There are also friends to be met who have been shipmates onboard other schooners, or from other places.

Mackerel netting did not keep my thoughts away from international racing. I hoped to take part in it so, naturally, I followed events and was not surprised when news came of Angus Walter's announcement that *Gilbert Walters* would sail under a new skipper next season. He was negotiating for the building of a new vessel at the yard of Smith and Rhuland, Lunenburg. Rumour also mentioned the Shelburne Shipyards would soon lay a keel for a potentially 'better than average' sailer, to be launched in time for a season on the banks. This was one of the required qualifications for competitors for The Halifax Herald Trophy.

All this activity made designers interested. They became involved. Usually, the master builder in any of the Nova Scotia yards that built wooden vessels was a designer in his own right. Not only could he design but he could also make the necessary alterations to a design, as required. It is safe to say a good many of the Nova Scotia schooners were the result of a half-model, carved from pinewood pieces cut to scale thickness, screwed together and carved to shape. When the designer was satisfied with the curves, diagonals, section lines etc., the cross station lines were established and numbered. These formed a series from bow to stern. Then he would take the model apart and measure the size and shape of each individual frame, beam and carling. Some people believe in the philosophy that a ship is a calculated creation whose end result is not known until tested. This may be, but I have known of hundreds of half-models being carved out, upon which the builder relied entirely. The half-model would even show the water-line. When the finished product slid down the ways and settled in the water, the sea level and the water-line would parallel each other, which proved the person who had carved the model had talent and sufficient knowledge to shape the coefficient and buoyancy curves to the proper sequence.

By virtue of *Resolute's* victory over *Shamrock IV,* the 100 Guineas, or America Cup, was being held in the United States. In the winter of 1921, they also held The Halifax Herald Trophy. We had talked ourselves into this situation and, now, we would have to sail ourselves out of it.

Competition was open for half-models and offset tables. Experienced designers sharpened their pencils and honed their carving tools. Master builders not only worked on models themselves but, also, they were faced with the responsibility to judge and evaluate half-models and sail plans. They hoped a champion would emerge from these. It may seem odd that men who were actual competitors should also have the task of selecting a winner, but the urgency dictated drastic measures.

Eventually, Mr. W.J. Roue, manager of a ginger ale business in Halifax, presented the most attractive sail plan and hull design. The new vessel would be built by Smith and Rhuland and commanded by Captain Angus Walters. Right from the start, there were rumours that the long, sleek lines presented potential qualities, but, some people with authority were in doubt concerning some characteristics of the hull arrangement. This doubt was to haunt the choice until the vessel started to shape up and show her profile.

It was not too difficult for a highline Grand Bank salt fishing skipper to choose a suitable vessel. He would want a large seaworthy craft which he could fill with fish. Builders would agree. Also, the vessel must have the strength and ability to be hard pushed regardless of sea and weather conditions. To combine these qualities with speed demanded compromise. All this was held in mind when designing and building a new schooner to bring back The Halifax Herald

Trophy to Canada. However, priority must go to a sound economic venture, and the craft must be sturdy and able to bring her crew safely home from the restless and angry sea.

Something had now been started on the southeast coast of Canada and on the eastern seaboard of the United States, something which was beyond the wildest dreams of the shipbuilding industry. An international schooner race, spurred on by friendly rivalry and general interest, was going to be responsible for the building of, at least, six schooners in Nova Scotia, from 1920 to 1938. Boston and Gloucester were to see seven vessels built in the same period and for the same reason. All this activity was brought about in order to compete for The Halifax Herald Trophy. The winner of the Trophy could claim the honour of being the North Atlantic International Fishing Schooner Sailing Champion.

Soon after the Roue plans were accepted, the work began of laying the keel for Captain Walter's new schooner. The Duke of Devonshire, the Governor General of Canada, made a special trip from Ottawa and, in a colourful ceremony, drove the first spike. The building of the 121st schooner to be launched from the yards of Smith and Rhuland was now under way. Shipwrights lost no time in taking over the work of framing the new hull. Its name would be *Bluenose* and it would be 112' WL with 10,000 sq. ft of sail area. A massive accumulation of Nova Scotia grown timber would become another Grand Banker.

The work went on. *Bluenose* began to shape up. Many of the citizens of Lunenburg went frequently to the shipyards to watch the construction as it progressed. Lunenburgers are not easily deceived. Instinctively, they know what is best and won't settle for anything less.

They watched the gradual development of the vessel, gathered large bundles of chips and chunks of wood, and made the casual comment. This was normal routine for dorymen ashore.

Eventually, the casual comments turned into serious discussions. Their concern had also entered the thoughts of those who were interested for financial reasons. The more the frames of *Bluenose* shaped up, the greater the concerns became. Finally, the question was out in the open. "What kind of forecastle will the vessel have?"

Men who dress in oilskins go over the side in dories at 0600. At 2200, or 16 hours later, they are still at work, this time on deck, gutting and splitting fish. They have worn their oilskins all day. They deserve and need a well ventilated and spacious accommodation in which to eat and sleep. The forecastle of a dory fishing schooner housed 14 to 18 men. These same men come from neat, trim and comfortable homes. The schooners in which they choose to go out to the fishing banks must be the same as far as the forecastle is concerned.

Captain Walters and the senior shipwrights had also realized the situation. The forecastle would be low, dark and cramped compared to that of the big knockabout. In the latter, men could move freely and without interruption. The table setting alone would look after twelve men at a time, if need be. *Bluenose* must also have a roomy forecastle. If there was any such thing as signing a contract where Captain Walters was involved, the fine print would have to state, very clearly, that he was to get what he wanted. I knew him well enough for that.

That being the case, there was not any danger of conflict. It was decided an alteration should be made to *Bluenose's* bow, and that it be raised 18 inches. All those concerned agreed. Several of the frames were knocked down and reset, as required. When the time came for *Bluenose* to slide down the ways, she would have plenty of room in her forecastle. If the alteration did anything to slow her down, no one will ever know. There were enough sailing qualities in her to win back the Trophy and to defend it successfully for 18 years, until there were no more challengers to haunt her.

Bluenose was launched 26 March 1921. Immediately she was taken in hand by riggers to have her masts stepped, shrouds and stays fitted and secured, blocks and running rigging fastened on booms, gaffs and mastheads put in place and, finally, the sails bent on. In the meantime, a crew had been signed on under the supervision of an experienced second-hand or first mate. Trawl gear, dories and other associated gear, were rigged and ready to sail for the banks. This had been made possible because all those engaged in building and in getting her ready had stuck closely to a pre-arranged time table. The day had come for which all

Lunenburg seafaring citizens had been waiting. For the first time, they were able to see *Bluenose* manoeuvering under sail. Two other schooners got under way about the same time.

A couple of hours later, the three schooners were outside the harbour, heading out beyond the horizon. Observers, returning from various vantage points, agreed on what they had seen. *"Bluenose"*, they said, "manoeuvered exceptionally well and was sailing fast." This seemed to be the general comment all during the season. Whenever *Bluenose* and other schooners of the fleet joined company sailing about the Grand Bank, or sailing to Newfoundland ports for bait, she had no difficulty in outsailing the best of them. Interest and hope generated for the return of The Halifax Herald Trophy.

Meanwhile, in Essex, Mass., the schooner *Mayflower* was on the building stocks. She would have to make, at least, one trip to the banks in order to qualify for the series to be sailed off Halifax. The Halifax Herald Trophy regulations stipulated that those taking part in the race must be bona fide fishing schooners. Starling Burgess knew how to design a fast sailing vessel. *Mayflower* was large. She had good carrying capacity and was of strong construction. However, fate ruled she was too much of a yacht, in comparison with the conventional banker. This was strictly a matter of opinion. *Mayflower* never did get a chance to compete in a race. Had she done so, I cannot say how she would have fared, but I do say, "She was a pretty vessel and smart under sail."

There were no additional new fishing schooners built that winter in Mass. On 30 May 1921, *Esperanto,* while fishing off Sable Island, struck the sunken vessel *S/S State of Virginia* and sank in less than 30 minutes. The crew boarded the dories and saw *Esperanto* sink in eleven fathoms of water with 140,000 lbs. of salt cod onboard. There was a moderate southeast wind and the fog was thick. However, later that same day, the crew were picked up by the schooner *Elsie* and landed at Halifax, Nova Scotia.

Incidentally, later that fall, *Elsie* won the elimination contest off Gloucester and would replace *Esperanto* to defend the Trophy in a series off Halifax, in October.

While *Elsie* was being chosen in the Gloucester elimination races, Lunenburg was not taking anything for granted. It was decided to hold a series of races over the Halifax triangle.

Saturday, 15 October 1921, found eight Lunenburg salt-bankers manoeuvering for a good start across the line which ran between the Royal Nova Scotia Yacht Squadron and Ives Knoll buoy. Among those included was *Canadia*. She was brand new and a product of the Shelburne shipyards. She was large and able. Naturally, people wondered what sort of a show she would make in the race. *Delawana* and *Alcala* were entrants and, of course, *Bluenose*. Others were *Independence, J. Duffy, Ada Corkum* and *Donald Cook*, old seasoned bankers. These vessels, with their captains, could cope with a strong breeze.

The wind averaged 18 knots. *Bluenose* and *Canadia* demonstrated that the new construction and design resulted in faster vessels than the previously built contenders. *Bluenose* crossed the finish line four minutes and eight seconds ahead of *Canadia*. *Alcala* and *Delawana* were next. 49 minutes later, the last of them crossed the line, *J. Duffy* bringing up the rear.

On 17 October, the 25 knot *Ene* breeze was, pretty much, a repetition of the 15th. *Bluenose* came first, with *Delawana* 16 minutes later. This concluded the elimination race with encouraging hopes that the Trophy might be brought back to Canada.

On Tuesday, 18 October, at Halifax, two waterfront berthing facilities had been surveyed for underwater obstruction, or damaging objects, and had been reserved for *Bluenose* of Lunenburg and *Elsie* of Gloucester. In the meantime, *Elsie* was heading for Halifax under escort by a U.S.N. destroyer. Captain Marty and her crew would receive a warm welcome in appreciation of the effort and sportsmanship for choosing and rigging another entry to replace *Esperanto*.

By this time, *Bluenose* had been hauled out. She had her bottom cleaned and painted. In a fresh northwest wind, she sailed the 45 mile voyage to Halifax. To her surprise, she met up with the Boston schooner *Mayflower*. *Mayflower* had been down on the Cape Shore on a haddock trip, but had decided to take time out to see, at least, one race of the series. The two schooners were quite close, when about eight miles south of Betty's Island. *Bluenose* had her topsails and balloon set.

24

Mayflower had been struck down for winter fishing, with no topmasts and only four lowers set. However she also headed for the approaches to Halifax Harbour, then about 16 miles away. Gradually, she fell behind *Bluenose*. The crew aboard *Bluenose* had the feeling *Mayflower* was not being pushed at any time during the brief brush, and that it could not be called a test of their respective merits.

Mayflower accompanied *Bluenose* to the inner approaches of the harbour, giving a good account of herself when close-hauled. Later, members of the *Bluenose* crew were questioned on how the two schooners compared. Their answers were almost unanimous, "She stayed behind. Guess, maybe, they wanted to make us feel good."

During the next two days, citizens of Halifax spent much time down on the water-front, viewing the two lofty and trim Grand Bank fishing schooners. The general feeling about *Elsie* seemed to be "Don't under-estimate any Gloucester fishing schooner for its sailing qualities."

At this point, *Bluenose* was an unknown quantity. Even her builders had said, "She's different from other vessels we've built." If anyone had knowledge of her sailing qualities it would be Captain Angus Walters and the dorymen who had enjoyed a successful fishing season onboard her. They would only say, "She is a good all round vessel — goes to windward well."

Sailing schooners have their fancies. Some vessels sail faster in just a fresh breeze, possibly because of delicate stability. When careened to a greater angle by the wind and excessive sail area, her lines of least resistance are lost. It was soon discovered that *Bluenose* suffered little from that condition. She was better than average in a light wind. Also, she was able and fast in heavy wind and rough water. Sometimes, she rolled out a high windward side, but the leeward side had the buoyancy qualities to keep her on top with a dry deck. She could also be depended upon to respond to rudder alterations, if necessary, during a heavy gust. That is what the fishing crew meant when they described *Bluenose* as "a very good all round vessel." Most seagoing fishermen are moderate in their language and don't elaborate.

Chapter 2

On Saturday, 22 October 1921, at 0800, the weather conditions in the Halifax Harbour area were: wind northwest 25 knots, cloudy and cool.

Bluenose and *Elsie,* with four lowers and topsails set, were manoeuvering from starting gun position. Marty Welch got *Elsie* across the starting line a few seconds ahead of *Bluenose.* However, Angus had *Bluenose* in the weather position. In less than three miles, on the first leg, *Bluenose* sailed under the lee of *Elsie* and took the lead. The distance from the starting line to Shut-in Island buoy, over that particular triangle, is 21 nautical miles. The wind had increased to 27 knots. From the start of the course to the first marker was a reach of six miles; from the first marker to the second marker there was a six mile run; from the second marker to the third there was a run of nine miles. During that phase of the race, *Bluenose* continued to lead *Elsie* but, never at any time, were the two schooners more than one minute apart. *Bluenose* rounded the Shut-in Island buoy at 10 hrs 46' 49", *Elsie* at 10 hrs 47' 16". This was a good example of what two able schooners could do when driven before the wind. *Bluenose* had now proven that she had the qualities to compete with one of Gloucester's finest vessels, while running free. *Bluenose* would now be called upon to show her capabilities in windward work, during the next two hours. It would be her first test under stiff competition.

The wind had varied to west, and had settled down to a steady 27 knots with gusts to 35 knots. The captains and crews realized they were facing a new situation, during which the stress and strain is hard on rigging, canvas and masts. Anything is liable to happen. Everyone onboard had to be alert for 'circumstances'. It is a time when the man at the helm must be cool and competent. The foam crested 20 foot ocean swells are solid and powerful. The helmsman can help his boat meet them with limited ease, or allow her to drive into them. The later choice creates sudden jerk and strain which is hard on the gear.

Soon after rounding Shut-in buoy, and on the way back along the eleven mile beat to windward, the gap widened. *Bluenose* was pointing higher and sailing much faster. Also, she was coping with the wind and sea exceptionally well. Both vessels were under four lowers, staysail and main-topsail. Angus decided to try the ballooner. It was hoisted and sheeted in. It soon proved its worth for the speed increased and windward pointing improved. It had a lifting effect that was pulling her ahead and up to the windward.

Marty and his crew were quick to notice what was taking place. They answered by hoisting *Elsie's* ballooner but, unfortunately, her fore-topmast failed to take the strain and broke off a few feet above the mast-head. This made her slow down until the loose bits and pieces were cut adrift or secured down. Captain Walters, being the seaman and sportsman that he was, hauled down the ballooner and clewed up the fore-topsail. He thought this action to be the best and only thing he could do in order to finish the race on relative and equal footing.

From the time the two schooners rounded Shut-in Island buoy and until they crossed the finish line, *Bluenose* demonstrated her best sailing points. She could carry sail, go to windward and was fast. She made the eleven miles to windward in one tack less than *Elsie*. She crossed the finish line at 13 hrs 32' 10", for an average speed of 10.8 knots. *Elsie* crossed at 13 hrs 45' 25".

Monday, 24 October 1921, saw the wind coming from the NNW at 12 knots. The day was sunny, with good visibility. Mart got *Elsie* across the starting line about four lengths ahead of *Bluenose*. She maintained that lead for the 6.2 miles to the Inner Automatic buoy and for the 10.2 miles to the Lightship buoy. Rounding it, *Elsie* kept the lead down the broad reach of seven miles to the Outer Automatic buoy. At this point, Angus had *Bluenose* in the windward position and sufficiently close to blanket *Elsie*. *Bluenose* then took the weather position rounding the buoy. From then on, *Bluenose* took the lead for the remaining 12.2 miles of windward sailing and beat *Elsie* by slightly more than three miles to the finish line.

This was the first international contest for *Bluenose*. She had given a good account of herself. The Halifax Herald Trophy was back in Canada. *Bluenose* would be an able defender.

Had this event taken place forty years later, no doubt interested spectators would have enjoyed following the races over live T.V. However, the *Halifax Herald* rose to the occasion and rigged up overhead wires from their building to another building across Sackville Street. Two model schooners showed the relative positions of the racers, based on periodic information sent ashore from a Committee vessel accompanying *Bluenose* and *Elsie*. The Committee boat reported by wireless to the Camperdown W/T Station. From there, the messages were relayed by land phone to Halifax.

Immense crowds watched the progress of the models as they were jerked along on the overhead wires. On Argyle Street, and up and down Sackville Street, people craned their necks for hours. As some left, others took their places. That night, citizens of Halifax, along with many out of town people who filled the hotels to overflowing, were jubilant and in a celebrating mood. A goodly supply of liquid refreshment was delivered, gratuitously, to the schooners. Much of it was sparkling champagne. There is a story which keeps cropping up from time to time. It is said that during the wee hours of the morning, when about all the congratulatory booze had been consumed, one 'old salt' announced, "It's time we had a drink," and, forthwith, pulled the bung from a keg of black rum.

This concluded the International Fishermen's Schooner Races for 1921. The event had created the urge to design a yet faster vessel. This was upper-most in the minds of many of the capable fishing schooner designers. Gloucester was coming back with a new and fast vessel. The famous yards in Essex, Mass. would see to that. Lunenburg was always adding to its fleet. The new ones would still be fishing schooners but, like *Bluenose,* different and, if at all possible, faster.

It was agreed the 1922 series would be sailed in U.S waters and any future series would be on an alternating system, year and year about.

News from Gloucester reported the keel for a new Gloucesterman had been laid at the yard of Arthur D. Story. A 'McManus' design, the schooner would be named *Henry Ford.* Clayton Morrissey would be captian. Rumours also stated Boston enthusiasts would finance another schooner. When this became a reality, the gold lettered name board on her bow would read *Yankee.*

The 1922 salt fish fleet enjoyed a normal season. The highliners with their skippers, some of whom were called 'fish killers', returned with full loads, *Bluenose* included. The salt trips ranged from April until September. Times were changing, however, and many schooners were installing diesel engines, cutting down the masts, thus reducing the sail area. They would go winter fresh fishing, packing their catch in ice and returning to port every five to seven days. Dory fresh fishing is somewhat different to dory salt fish trawling. Winter conditions are also more difficult and hazardous and, to cope with the differences, auxiliary power driven schooners make it safer for the dorymen, and also more efficient for the scheduling of fresh fish landings.

Back in the shipyards in Mass., construction of *Yankee* and *Ford* had reached a date of completion in sufficient time to be on the fishing banks for, at least, one trip, thus qualifying to race for The Halifax Herald Trophy.

Yankee was a much smaller schooner than *Bluenose* or *Ford.* She was pretty and considered to be a very good all round fishing vessel. *Henry Ford* had the misfortune to be damaged at the time of her launching. This was not an unusual event. Once in a while, some hidden flaw in the launchways, or some other factor, will cause the vessel to 'act up'. She may hit the water in an awkward manner but no real harm occurs. However, should she fail to reach the water, damage does occur. *Ford's* repairs delayed her getting out on the fishing banks in sufficient time. The Racing Committee agreed, unanimously, that under the circumstances, *Ford* should not be prevented from competing as challenger should she qualify in elimination races.

The U.S. Committee scheduled an elimination series to be sailed over the Cape Ann triangle, 12 October to 14 October. The entries were: *L.A. Dunton, Elizabeth Howard, Henry Ford* and *Yankee.* The last two were trim and fast fishermen of unknown qualities. *Henry Ford* was the winner and was chosen to prepare to meet *Bluenose* in home waters over the Cape Ann triangle. The first race was to be on 21 October.

In the meantime, *Bluenose, Canadia, Mahaska* and *Margaret K. Smith* were competing 'Down East', as Gloucestermen say. They were using the Halifax triangle. *Bluenose* had to defend her honour against two new schooners. The *Smith* was only a couple of years old. It was expected the contest would be interesting. *Mahaska* was built to be fast. *Canadia,* from the Shelburne builders, was not to be underestimated, and *Margaret K. Smith* had already established herself as a good sailer. *Mahaska* was built for Captain Paddy Mack.

I've heard stories of Paddy's interest for able and fast vessels. A schooner, *Clintonia,* built in Essex, Mass., in 1907, had turned out to be a very good all round vessel. Her graceful lines and attractive sail plan took Captain Paddy's eye, so much so, that the very next year a Canadian *Clintonia* was launched from Smith and Rhuland yards at Lunenburg. It was of the same model and copied all the characteristics of the Essex boat. Captain Mack took her salt fishing and landed several good catches. So there was general interest to see how *Mahaska* would fare.

There are certain traditions and beliefs which fishermen hold fast. Examples are: "Don't go onboard a fishing schooner wearing coloured mittens"; and, certain words must be left ashore. But, by the same token, other things are accepted as symbols of good fortune. Fishermen have faith in a name in which three 'A's are used. This was done with the names *Mahaska* and *Canadia.* No fisherman would admit this was superstition. Whether it was or not is of small consequence, for it did not work. Neither of these vessels could cause the average salt-banker much concern when it came to all round fast sailing.

Bluenose won the race of 7 October 1922. A second race, scheduled for Monday, 9 October, was called off, due to very light winds. There was no doubt *Bluenose* was the best schooner. She was also the defender. Unanimously, the Committee agreed that the 1922 Canadian elimination series be ended and that *Bluenose* be awarded first place. *Bluenose* returned to Lunenburg for docking, cleaning and painting, and then proceeded on her way to Gloucester.

As a formal gesture, a Canadian naval vessel was invited to visit the port in the capacity of an official escort. Also, there was a Department of Marine and Fisheries vessel, having onboard Committee members, press representatives and associated business personnel, whose presence may, or may not, be required during the contest. International events, regardless of their nature of friendliness, will, occasionally, call for diplomatic assistance.

The American Race Committee had confirmed that the schooner *Henry Ford* would be the U.S. challenger. Both vessels were notified they were to be ready to commence the series on 21 October.

Captain Clayton Morrissey and Captain Angus Walters were two highline fishing captains. They were old acquaintances. They knew and understood each other. It would be man against man, and schooner against schooner. In spite of their rivalry, there would be no unfair procedures and dishonest manoeuvering, nor argument between these two men. Each had the qualities and honour to be captains of the fastest and ablest two-masted fishing schooners ever built. They took great personal pride in their positions and were more than anxious to get the contest started. This strong desire to be under way was responsible for an unauthorized start of the first race.

Walters and Morrissey were setting sails and manoeuvering the schooners to be in correct position to cross the line at the starting gun, when the Committee, believing the wind was too light, decided to postpone the start for half an hour. A postponement signal was hoisted but the two schooners, less than mainboom length apart, were now heading across the starting line, with all sails set. The two captains saw the signal, but they were convinced they should start the race. They regarded themselves as 'masters of their own destiny'. The two vessels were sailing so closely to each other that there was no need to shout. The captains exchanged a few brief words and agreed to carry on. 'Carry on' is a common phrase among seamen. They hate to turn back.

The Committee did not have that tradition in their blood. As far as they were concerned, there was no race. *Bluenose* and *Ford* sailed on. The Canadian destroyer closed each vessel and delivered a verbal message from the Committee, reiterating the fact that the race was postponed. It made no difference. Clayton and Angus were racing the two vessels over the Cape Ann triangle in the light wind. In the end, it required more than six hours to complete the course. *Henry Ford* held the lead all the way.

Two strikes were against the two captains for (a) an unauthorized start, and (b) time limit overlap. Captain Walters said, "It's a race for Clayton." The Comittee said 'No race'. The crews were angry and ready to quit. Finally, the Secretary of the Navy stepped in and calm was restored, thanks to the respect which the dory fishermen had for their brothers in 'blue'. It was doubtful if they would have listened to anyone else.

The next race was sailed in light wind and, again, *Ford* crossed the finish line first, almost two minutes over the six hour time limit. Legally, it was not a race. In the minds of the skippers, it was a fair race. This was sufficient, as far as they were concerned. A couple of minutes at the end of a fair competition could not destroy the principles of these two men. Remarks under "Voice of the People" columns, and discussions in the bars, revealed mixed feelings. Some maintained "It only required two races to win."

Many fishermen were aware the light winds of the past two days could not continue. When this happens off Cape Ann in October, it is called a 'weather breeder'. Strong winds would come and *Bluenose* would be able to show her mettle. During the next two races, the wind velocity exceeded 25 knots and

Bluenose was able to demonstrate her excellent qualities as an able and fast vessel. She had no difficulty in carrying all sail and winning by a safe margin. In turn, *Ford* suffered a broken topmast and was unable to stay with *Bluenose* when it blew hard.

This concluded the 1922 series. *Bluenose* returned home to Lunenburg with the Trophy and prize money. The crew assembled at the Bandstand on Town Square, where they received congratulations and heard appreciative remarks. Then they returned to the schooner. In all probability, they were told to drop into the Company office to receive some small token of esteem. In the life of a doryman, this had been a month of unique seafaring.

A few days later, most of the men were back to work. Some went to the West Indies. Some sailed to Mediterranean ports. They would deliver a load of dried cod fish and return home with a cargo of salt or molasses. Others went back to the dories and winter fresh fishing in the hope of replenishing their bank accounts. Meandering ashore in Boston or Halifax will cause deep scars to a limited savings account.

Citizens of the New England States are extremely interested in sailing craft. They build good, fast and able vessels. *Ford* was good, but not good enough, so they must try again. Starling Burgess was asked to design a vessel suitable for engaging in both salt and fresh fishing. Also, she must be a fast all round sailer. As a result, *Columbia* was launched from A.D. Story yard in Essex, Mass., in the early spring of 1923.

When they saw her for the first time, fishermen said, "She is a beautiful vessel." She had a trim hull and a large sail area plan. She was rated as a fast boat by fishermen returning from the banks. Early in the season, *Columbia* was looked upon as the challenger. However, the Committee was not going to take it for granted, and insisted an elimination race be sailed over the Cape Ann triangle, 21 October.

Columbia, Elizabeth Howard and *Henry Ford* went over the course. *Columbia* outsailed *Ford* and *Howard* on all points and was confirmed as the challenger. Ben Pine would be the racing skipper and several other Gloucester fishing skippers would be onboard as crew members. Ben had undergone his initiation as schooner racing captain onboard

Elizabeth Howard during the elimination races. He now had the honour to take the new challenger to Canadian waters, and to meet *Bluenose*.

That event became a reality, 29 October 1923. Pine had seen *Bluenose* in all the previous contests and was aware of her qualities. Angus Walters sized up *Columbia* and, no doubt, was conservative in his outward remarks. He knew she would be fast, but would that be true under all sailing conditions? *Columbia* had a large and beautiful set of sails.

Bluenose arrived at the starting line somewhat lighter in ballast than for her previous races. The under water sections of her hull had absorbed much salt water since her launching. It was added weight but it was properly distributed.

The starting gun on the morning of 29 October sent the two schooners off in a moderate westerly wind. It was not the kind of weather *Bluenose* would have chosen, but she was alive and on her way. She crossed the line a length ahead of *Columbia*. For the next couple of hours it was 'nip and tuck'. The two boats stayed close to each other. The wind had increased to a fresh WSW breeze. A luffing match developed, soon after turning the third marker, and while heading back to Halifax Harbour. *Columbia* was out under the lee bow of *Bluenose* and kept pushing her to windward, rather than allow her to blanket and sail out ahead. This is a good tactic if it can be made to work, otherwise, it is a waste of valuable time. *Columbia* continued to be unyeilding. She forced *Bluenose* close to shallow water, for the second time. According to the law of the sea, *Bluenose* was privileged to take any action which would prevent her from going ashore. Suddenly, *Columbia* found herself in an awkward position. She must either get out of the way or suffer the consequences. It was too late to get entirely out of the way. *Bluenose* had *Columbia* blanketed and was holding her course, at an estimated speed of nine knots. The end of her mainboom ravaged the rigging of the challenger. Sheer poles were ripped off and bent, wire stretched and rendered free. For a brief period, *Bluenose*'s mainboom threatened to leave the saddle, until several of the crew threw in their weight to prevent it happening. Finally, *Bluenose* was past and clear of *Columbia*'s forerigging shrouds, but she hooked a bight of a jib downhaul rope and

34

pulled the challenger for a short distance. *Bluenose* was to windward, on course, and picking up speed. The rope failed to stress and parted. Then *Bluenose* sailed away from *Columbia* and on to the finish line, nine miles away. Up to this time, it was believed the weather conditions favoured *Columbia*.

Controversy raged that evening on the waterfront. The respective merits of the two schooners were compared. *Columbia* had been designed to be fast. She had lived up to those expectations and, particularly so, on some relative angles to the wind. On the other hand, *Bluenose* was fast and better than average on all relative angles to the wind. In addition to that, she was able. W.J. Roue and George Rhuland had produced something unique in fishing schooners. People wondered if anyone else would get all the components in the same balanced sequence again.

Moderate winds delayed the next race for a couple of days. Captain Pine and the crew of *Columbia* made good use of the extra time. They worked on the ballast in the hope that changing the trim, or water-line length, might help.

The Committee would have done well if they had spent the intervening time playing golf. Instead, they sat down and messed around with the rules. They made an amendment concerning 'aid to navigation buoys', saying these must be passed on a certain side. This addition to the rules was made in order to discourage luffing matches. The buoys would be the scapegoats. No doubt, the amendment was delivered onboard the respective schooners, but here the matter stopped. A routine Government Marine Notice to Mariners making reference to buoys, chart corrections and things of that nature, would receive necessary and prompt attention. 'Aid to navigation buoys' and 'race course marker buoys' are two different things. The captains were concerned with the latter set. They would treat 'aid to navigation buoys' in the normal way.

The moderate winds of the past two days developed into a gusty northeaster on the morning of 1 November. The breeze was strong enough to make the scuppers awash, while manoeuvering for the start. *Bluenose* swung off and crossed the line pretty much on the extreme east end, a few seconds after the gun, but a couple of schooner lengths ahead of

Columbia who was on the west end of the line. Each schooner set a course directly at the first marker, six miles before the wind. The vessels were one quarter of a mile apart, or approximately so. This position caused *Bluenose* to pass Light House Bank buoy off to starboard. *Columbia* passed the same buoy off to port. There was no interference or advantage of any sort. In fact, *Bluenose* would be travelling a greater distance. Angus had regarded the buoy as an 'aid to navigation', and had treated it in the normal fashion. *Bluenose* led all the way. *Columbia* trailed, but was never more than three minutes behind at any time. *Columbia's* average speed was about 8.7 knots, taking windward work into consideration.

Each vessel crossed the finish line, lowered away and furled sails. They accepted the services of tugboats for berthing, and regarded the series as ended, *Bluenose* being the winner and defender of the Trophy. Then, after they were secured in their berths, the news broke that Pine was protesting on the buoy technicality. He was justified, according to the amended rules.

The Committee spent several hours before making an announcement. Finally, it came. The race was awarded to *Columbia*.

The crew of *Bluenose* felt they had won the two races in a fair and square manner. It was folly to think they would agree to the decision of the Committee. Possibly, they might have been persuaded to race again if the contest had been called 'no race'. But that did not happen and *Bluenose* got ready to sail for home. *Columbia* was awarded half the prize money and returned to Gloucester. The trophy remained with *Bluenose* and she returned to Lunenburg.

People who had followed the races had the opportunity to make an assessment of the two schooners, and the problems which the captains had to face. Seamanship tactics, wind, sea, visibility, constant attention to sails and rigging create great demands on any captain. In addition, these captains were burdened with the extra responsibility of making a special courtesy to harbour channel buoys. No wonder things ended in controversy, through no desire of their own. There was frustration, so much so, that it was eight years before another international race was held for The Halifax Herald Trophy.

36

Chapter 3

Between 1923 and 1931 great changes took place in the fishing fleets of Lunenburg and Gloucester.

The alterations made during the construction of *Bluenose* were still being talked about. Curiosity concerning their effect continued to obsess designers and builders. In 1924, a group of Halifax citizens and Bill Roue, the designer, decided to build a schooner that might sail faster than *Bluenose*. The Shelburne yards were given the order and, in the spring of 1925, a large, sleek, lofty vessel, named *Haligonian*, was launched. Moyle Crouse, of Lunenburg, would be her captain. *Haligonian* would be somewhat lower forward and was not to undergo alterations for forecastle accommodation.

By now, it was certain there would be a race in Canadian waters, mainly to satisfy curiosity about the design of *Haligonian*. She would spend the spring and summer out on the Grand Bank, salt fishing. During that time, plans would be made for a contest off Halifax, in October.

The Grand Bank of Newfoundland, the Sable Island banks and the Nova Scotia coast are noted for prolonged periods of fog, caused by the Arctic waters coming from the north mingling with the waters of the Gulf Stream coming from the south. The miserable wet air often reduced the visibility to 60 yards and continued that way for weeks. Many of the schooners had made good catches down on the Grand

Bank, approximately 450 miles from Lunenburg. They were working back nearer to the Nova Scotia coast where they would call in at bait supply ports. After taking on fresh bait, they would return to the Gulf of St. Lawrence or to the Sable Island banks and top off the catch.

Haligonian sailed for days through the fog and arrived at the rock strewn entrance to Canso. She heard the fog alarm horn on Cranberry Island and proceeded towards the inner harbour. About half-way in, she had the misfortune to go aground on a gravel reef. She was refloated a couple of days later, but being heavily loaded with salt cod fish, there was the possibility that her hull might be strained and twisted.

Bluenose had a similar experience on the coast of Newfoundland. She struck a rock shoal and was holed. She was refloated and taken to a Newfoundland port. She was repaired sufficiently to make her safe for the voyage home to Lunenburg, about 600 miles away.

Bluenose and *Haligonian* were damaged. Time would be required to make permanent repairs after the load of salt fish was delivered at Lunenburg. There was no sense in thinking about a race for 1925, not even an exhibition one.

The spring and summer of 1926 came and went. There were good catches, no hurricanes and no groundings. A series of exhibition races was scheduled for October. The races would be over the Halifax triangle and a test would be made to see if the design of *Haligonian* was superior to that of *Bluenose*.

On 15 October 1926 both vessels arrived in Halifax, ready to go. The event was concluded 20 October, after the schooners had completed four engagements. Two of the races were sailed in light wind and did not finish within the time limit. The other two races were sailed under varying weather conditions, but were finished in time. *Bluenose* was a comfortable winner. *Haligonian* had her sails cut and the ballast shifted but, in no way, did her sailing qualities compare with *Bluenose*.

The autumn hurricane of 1927 swept over the Atlantic Canadian shelf, leaving in its wake death and destruction. Several U.S. and Canadian schooners were missing with all hands. The list included *Columbia*. The surviving vessels made port minus gear, dories and other equipment and, in some cases, even the sails and booms were gone. The crews had to make jury-rigs which eventually brought them back home. *Bluenose* lost all her deck gear and dories. She was hove down to her sheer poles. As a result, about eight feet of water kept pouring over her deck. When the sea becomes so furious and destructive, the qualities of both men and ship are tested. After the ordeal was over, many people said of *Bluenose*, "It's a miracle the vessel could stand it." That statement was well founded.

Fascination for the sea and the urge to practise a fishing career overruled the distress caused by the recent grim experience. The schooners were repaired. Dories were replaced and new vessels built. Off to the banks they went. In keeping with all this was the same recurring hope that some. time, and some how, a challenger would come to revive 'the race'.

Boston racing enthusiasts had the same hope. They, also, wanted another contest and they wanted it to be sailed off Boston. The enthusiasm reached a peak in 1929. With *Columbia* gone, Paine, Belknap and Skene, Naval Architects, were commissioned to design a bona fide fishing schooner that, hopefully, would be an interesting challenger. This effort to revive the international contest received wonderful support when *Bluenose* agreed to race for the Lipton Cup.

This cup had been given to Gloucester by Sir Thomas Lipton some time previously. The deed of gift stipulated that Gloucester fishing schooners should compete for it during the Annual Fiesta. In 1930, Gloucester would be celebrating her 300th anniversary. The deed of gift was altered in order to allow outside entries, and the Racing Committee invited *Bluenose* to take part.

The Paine, Belknap and Skene boat was built at Essex, 1929. She was named *Gertrude L. Thebaud*, being another very handsome Yankee fishing vessel. *Thebaud* proved herself to be a good all round fishing schooner during the winter of 1929-1930, when she went haddocking. She also went on a salt trip during the following summer.

The challenge having been issued and accepted, there would now be a contest between *Bluenose* and *Gertrude L.*

Thebaud for the Lipton Cup. The opening date was set for 9 October 1930.

Bluenose had accepted the challenge in spite of the fact that she was beginning to show weather beaten scars after ten full years of rugged Grand Bank fishing activity, and had worked off the northwest bar of Sable Island in a gale, and had been grounded on the rocks of Placentia Bay. The invitation would give *Bluenose* an opportunity to size up *Thebaud*, and this is what she wanted.

The enthusiasm may have been a bit low in Lunenburg while *Bluenose* was being prepared for the Gloucester event, particularly, when it was only to be an exhibition race. However, a good crew would go, and a new suit of sails was bent on. Then she left Lunenburg with a windy marine forecast which actually developed. It drove her across the Bay of Fundy to Gloucester in record time, to say nothing of what happened to the new suit of cotton canvas sails. It was not the first suit of sails to be initiated by wind, rain and salt spray. Undoubtedly, the result would show up during the contest because the sails were stretched out of shape.

The wind was light for the first race. *Gertrude L. Thebaud* looked trim, manoeuvered well and sailed well. *Bluenose* had all the appearance of a fishing schooner making a berth out on the banks, where little concern is given to the manner in which the sails set. She manoeuvered in a slow and awkward way.

Captain Ben Pine put *Thebaud* across the starting line well ahead of *Bluenose*. He maintained the lead, increased it and brought *Gertrude L. Thebaud* across the finish line to win the first race by a comfortable margin.

That evening, sail makers went to work on *Bluenose*. They shortened bolt rope and cut canvas. The next day, *Bluenose* was hauled out on the slipway to have her keel surface 'smoothed up'.

On Saturday, she came up to the starting line looking much more like her old self. Her sails were greatly improved and they handled much better, but they were not the sails for windward work. That day, and on the following Monday, the wind was light and the race had to be called off.

Then, on 15 October, there was a moderate gale from

the southeast, with rain. Previously, Captain Walters had stated *Bluenose* needed a blow. Captain Pine was of the opinion *Thebaud* could take good care of herself if it blew hard. The Committee boat started them off on schedule, in a gusty 30 knot wind, with rain squalls.

For the first time in the series, *Bluenose* was in charge. The strong wind and choppy waters were her delight. There was no problem working on deck and she was going fast. On board *Thebaud* it was different. She was losing time and dropping behind. In the first hour, *Bluenose* had established a two mile lead and was having no trouble with the wind and sea. However, the rain squalls reduced visibility to less than one-half mile, at times. The marker buoys were not the regular type of Coast Guard aids to navigation. Instead, they were of flag and staff construction. The Committee came to the conclusion they would be difficult to find and called the race off.

Captain Charlie Johnson was in command of *Thebaud*, as Captain Pine had been required to stay on shore. Charlie returned to Gloucester and had very little comment. Captain Walters was upset. *Bluenose* had been comfortable and sailing well. Angus had been willing to take his chances on finding the Baby Buoys, a label which the race crews had given them. This was a loss of valuable time to the crew. However, one thing had been proved. When there was a strong wind, *Bluenose* was a better sailer than *Thebaud*.

It was 18 October before there was enough wind to sail again. This time, it was light and 'shifty'. Even though it was light, *Bluenose* took the lead. Charlie Johnson was familiar with freaky wind games in this area, and was willing to let Angus split tacks. What Johnson expected, worked. Eventually, he got an advantageous wind slant, eased sheet, and sailed over the finish line well in the lead. This made *Thebaud* winner of the Lipton Cup.

The outcome of the Lipton series created renewed interest in favour of another international series for The Halifax Herald Trophy, but where were all the schooners and the schooner crewmen? Diesel motors had replaced sails. Mechanized draggers presented an entirely new hull profile. *Bluenose* and *Thebaud* were about the only remaining lofty schooner-rig boats operating in the Gloucester and Lunenburg fleets. The need for an elimination series was gone.

The way in which *Thebaud* won the Lipton Cup, in October 1930, was not sufficient proof she was faster than *Bluenose*. One race of the series had been a straight win. Another race had been won on a split tack manoeuver. Then there was the southeaster and rain squalls. In actual fact, there had not been a race of merit. Certainly, there was reason to form a committee which would co-ordinate a series for October 1931. *Gertrude L. Thebaud* would be the challenger. The race would be off Halifax. Hopefully, it would pick up and complete what *Bluenose* and *Columbia* had failed to finish in October 1923.

Bluenose returned from the Grand Bank during September, unloaded her catch and was turned over to the shipyards for cleaning, painting and to get the under water bumps dubbed to a smooth surface. The sailmaker went over the sails. Then came October. The racing schooners became the water-front topic and made the press headlines in Halifax, after a long absence of eight years.

Bluenose was looking good. She appeared to be taking pride in her tarnished rigging, work deck, seasoned topsides, polished and worn belaying pins. They were the accumulation of fair wear and tear after ten years on the fishing banks. All the under water portion of her hull was saturated with heavy sea-water. Yet, when she was secured to the jetty, in perfectly calm water, she could be seen doing a miniature pitch and roll and, occasionally, the mooring lines would moan with strain. She seemed to have a built-in urge to be under way and moving.

Gertrude L. Thebaud, a bona fide fishing vessel, arrived in Halifax beautifully turned out. She was tuned up as though she were brand new. Two years on the banks, under normal conditions, just about gets things in good shape.

The first race got under way on the morning of 17 October, in a light breeze. The wind failed to freshen during the day. However, *Bluenose* was less than a mile from the finish line when the time expired. *Thebaud* was a considerable distance behind. Two days later, with a fresh breeze, good visibility and smooth water, *Bluenose* led *Thebaud* on all legs of the triangle, and crossed the finish line almost three miles ahead.

42

Thebaud had made the trip from Gloucester to Halifax in about 36 hours. That was very good time and there was every reason to believe she was in racing trim. People could be excused for thinking so, but it now seemed as if something was off balance, somewhere. Could the sails have been stretched? Did she have too much ballast? Was she out of trim? Ben Pine and his crew realized something was wrong and made some changes which they hoped would improve *Thebaud's* performance.

On 20 October, the wind was from the west at 16 to 20 knots. The visibility was good and the sea was smooth. *Thebaud* appeared to be handling well, when manoeuvering for the start. She was smarter than she had been in Monday's race.

Bluenose was not heavily ballasted. She was fast and handling well. There was only a few seconds' difference in the start. For the next 14 miles, both vessels sailed side by side and eased sheets. At times, they were so close to each other that it was possible to exchange a plug of tobacco or to hear a friendly remark from a rival crewman.

Then came windward work and a slight change in wind velocity. *Bluenose* was living up to her well known tactic. She was pointing high and sailing away from her challenger. For a while, her speed was estimated at 9.5 knots. From then on, the race was not a serious contest. *Thebaud* was almost two miles behind when *Bluenose* crossed the finish line. The 1931 series was over. *Bluenose* was the faster and rightful custodian of The Halifax Herald Trophy.

Mahaska, Henry Ford, Canadia, Yankee, Columbia, Haligonian and *Gertrude L. Thebaud* were designed to be true fishing schooners. In addition to this, they were built to be faster than *Bluenose* and to beat her. Each, in turn, failed.

When the finishing touches are being applied to a new schooner, ready for launching, the supervising shipwrights are asked a common question, "What is this one going to be like?" When it was asked of *Bluenose*, the reply was, "She will be all right, but she is a bit different to most vessels." Ten years later, sailing fans, builders and designers, agreed she was different and, indeed, all right. She was the ideal of being different.

The people who were involved in designing, building

and sailing schooners suddenly realized the series just concluded could, possibly, be the end of the international races. Also, the fans were aware the schooner-rig vessel was no longer in demand in the fishing fleet. Furthermore, when a Grand Bank fishing schooner reaches ten years, she is likely to be sold. She may end up under Newfoundland Registry to be employed in the Labrador fishery, or in the coastal trade. This was not a happy thought.

Gertrude L. Thebaud was a beautiful vessel. It would take much to get her away from the State of Massachusetts. *Bluenose* had become a legend worthy of recognition. Surely, that recognition was beyond a price tag pay-off. Such a thing would never happen if Captain Angus Walters would prevent it. Angus was attached to *Bluenose*, so much so, that he understood all her ways. I think they could talk to each other. He was able to recognize the slightest peculiar move and to respond with the necessary action.

This 1931 series was the easiest, as far as the Sailing Committee was concerned. Weather conditions were good and the sailing routine went smoothly. It should not be thought that arguments which had arisen in the past had been with intent, or to create harassment. At certain times, when sudden incidents occur, rules, as such, have to go by the board. Decisions have to be made instantly, in order to cope with special situations. The captain makes them.

With the series over, each man returned to his work. It would vary from previous years but it would be related to deep sea fishing. Some went on the dragger type boats which had supplanted the hook and line method. Some regretted the old way was disappearing, but they realized there was a blessing in it. It was a relief to the men who used to go out in the dories. Now they were free from that hazardous practice peculiar to the winter months.

Champion *Bluenose* —
World's Fair, Chicago - Toronto, 1920
(Maritime Museum of the Atlantic Photo)

Captain Angus Walters

Seven schooners racing Halifax Harbour, October 1921 —
Independence, Alcala, Bluenose, Canadia, Delewana, J. Duffy, Ada Corkum

Captain Walters with Fisherman's trophy

Lunenburg Harbour 1905

Racing in full sail

Gertrude L. Thebaud

Columbia

Esperanto

Bluenose trails in
Henry Ford's lee off
Gloucester, Mass.

Elsie

Chapter 4

The future was uncertain for the two lofty windjammer schooners. Eventually, fate ruled they should become exhibition material and take part in outstanding world attractions, such as those which would be appropriate to their backgrounds.

In the city of Chicago, on the shores of Lake Michigan, preparations were well advanced for the Chicago Exposition. The Exposition was 1500 miles inland from the Grand Bank and Atlantic coast. *Gertrude L. Thebaud* and *Bluenose* were invited to attend and be one of the main attractions. The voyage would be unique for a Grand Bank fishing schooner. There would be the sail up the St. Lawrence River, passing the old city of Quebec and leaving behind the last taste of salt water. From Montreal, they would sail into Lake Ontario and pass through the Welland Canal to Lake Erie. From there they would go through Lake St. Clair into Lake Huron. Finally, they would pass through the Machinac Strait into Lake Michigan and on to Chicago.

The schooners proved to be a tremendous attraction. People were astonished at their size and type of rigging.

After Chicago, *Bluenose* sailed to Toronto and remained in that port all winter and into the spring. Here, she was open for sightseeing and sailing excursions, as weather permitted. *Bluenose* then returned to Lunenburg in the summer of 1934.

Soon after her return home, her owners were approached with an invitation to be present at Spithead for the 1935 Sailpast Review. They were also invited to take part in a yacht race around the Isle of Wight. There, she would be in company with the fast schooner yacht *Westward*. It was a great honour to be stationed among a flotilla of ships marking the Silver Jubilee of the coronation of their Majesties King George V and Queen Mary.

The ships sailed over the old established course which encircles the Isle of Wight. For *Bluenose*, it was more of a courtesy than a contest. However, many sailing and yachting people were astonished to see she had sufficient speed to keep her in close company with the large and fast racing yachts.

Although far from the Grand Bank and the Halifax or Gloucester triangles, *Bluenose* displayed the same excellent qualities. This vessel, with above average coefficient, and rigged with heavy cotton canvas sails, was still a joy to behold. *Bluenose* received a reward for the part she played for sailing around the Isle of Wight. King George gave her the lighter and specially stitched mainsail from the Royal Yacht *Britannia*.

A very unfortunate event happened within 24 hours of leaving the shores of the United Kingdom. On 17 September, she had left the port of Falmouth despite the fact there was a heavy gale warning in effect. Significance of the warning had been underestimated, and *Bluenose* found herself in the teeth of hurricane force winds. It was three days before the storm began to subside. By now, the hull was damaged and *Bluenose* had sprung a leak. She was obliged to return and put in at Plymouth. There she stayed for a month until the repairs were completed. That delayed her arrival home until 4 November. Again, after a rough voyage, if was necessary she be docked for immediate and complete caulking. Captain Walters described the hurricane as being much worse than the one off the northwest bar of Sable Island, in 1926. Her hull was strained and, no doubt, hogged from extreme pounding and stress.

In 1936, Angus was obliged to have engines installed. The topmasts were struck down and *Bluenose* was outfitted with twelve dories to go winter fishing. Whenever weather conditions permitted, she made trips of ten days duration, bringing back iced fresh fish.

It required careful planning to make the decision and to install engines. What was the best way to do it? When *Bluenose* was built, no provision had been made in the design and specifications for shaft logs and propellers. If there had been, it is likely one engine would have been the choice. In that case, the sensible thing would be to avoid interference by altering the stern post sections, or the rudder, in order to place the propeller. However, there was the possibility another sailing contest could develop. Finally, it was decided to install twin engines, with shaft logs out through the hull planking, port and starboard. The propellers would be placed down close to the rudder. One would turn left and the other right, in order to give the rudder an even transverse thrust. It was not the most economical arrangement, not the most efficient, but it meant the engines could be removed in their entirety should *Bluenose* be called upon to race again.

Profits were very low from fresh fish landings. There was too great a dependency on U.S. and local markets. Added to this, the volume of landings was high. The cure was to develop and increase sales on foreign markets, but these had been neglected. Also wood constructed schooner hulls deteriorate when laid up in a stagnant condition. The life of such vessels is preserved and prolonged by constantly being saturated with clean salt water, while at sea, and by the circulation of air, generated by the motion of the vessels. In order to preserve what was left, crewmen were being employed, but only at an existence wage. Dividends from the investment varied and were small, but the schooners were kept in good condition and operative, with the hope the economy would improve.

During such an era, managing owners were subjected to great pressure. Shareholders would rather sell at market price than pay for routine maintenance or, possibly, deficit operations. *Bluenose* had repaid her shareholders well. However, when the financial slump came, they wanted to sell. Of all the masters faced with this dilemma, Captain Walters was unique. He believed *Bluenose* would become part of Canadian seafaring history, and he believed the time would come soon when some Government Department would be ready and willing to provide a registered berth, alongside a museum jetty, for the Queen of the Atlantic Schooners. So strongly did he believe this that he and two other shareholders became sole owners of *Bluenose*. Angus held the majority of shares by a wide margin, thus taking the greatest part of the financial load.

In 1938 there was a temporary glimmer of relief. It did not come from the hoped for museum project, but from the initiative of those who sought to promote an international race. They wanted to revive the racing atmosphere and to satisfy Boston's long expressed wish to have the race sailed off that port. Also, it would remind the public that *Bluenose* and *Thebaud* were afloat and active.

Bluenose was now 18 years old. She had defended the Trophy since 1921. She was weather beaten and weary. Would it be wise to race? Financially, would it be worth while? The United States held the America Cup (the 100 Guineas Cup) and the Lipton Cup. Could the much younger and trim *Thebaud* capture The Halifax Herald Trophy? This was something to think about. Then there was the prize money of $3,000.00 and $2,000.00 for first and second places. Also, there would be a substantial bonus purse for each schooner, which would help to defray the additional expenses. Eventually, negotiations were completed. The U.S. Committee arranged the sailing schedule and courses. This time, Boston would be included. The Cape Ann triangle and the Boston course would be used alternately. The Boston course was a triangle off Cape Nahant. The series would be scheduled for October 1938. The first schooner to win three races would be awarded The Halifax Herald Trophy.

There was a great deal of work to be done by the riggers and crew of *Bluenose*. They rummaged the sail loft and spar yard to find the topmasts, light sails and associated blocks, sheets and downhauls and gear that had been stored away three years before. When all the gear was fitted in the original positions, it was found that the hull was hogged and that it was a bit soft, in places.

Work had progressed well during the last week of September and *Bluenose* was ready for the voyage to Gloucester. The engines would remain intact until after arrival in that port. They would be taken out when it was certain there

48

were no hitches and the race was confirmed. Also, there were 40 tons of iron ballast bars onboard. This would be enough to compensate for the weight of the engines and component parts, which would go ashore before the race.

The captain has a responsibility to Customs Excise and Immigration before leaving port on any voyage. He has to go to the clearance clerk at the local Customs House to take out a clearance permit. His ship must have a good 'Bill of Health', hull inspection certificate, crew list, articles relating to the nature of the voyage, the official registry, the tonnage, registered owners, the captain's nationality and official number. So it is necessary for the captain and crew to report to the Shipping Master's office and sign on as such. These documents are required so that, on arrival in a foreign port, the vessel may be granted a free partake.

That chore having been completed, we returned onboard and, by noon, 29 September, were under way and bound for Gloucester. Although I never heard it expressed out loud, I felt that each man aboard was greatly concerned about defending the Trophy.

An overcast sky, with increasing southeast wind, told us what to expect for the next 24 hours. That afternoon, with every stitch of canvas set, the increasing wind gave the crew an opportunity to adjust the sheets and lanyards, and to reset shackles and eyebolts. By 1800, the wind was estimated to be 20 knots. The four lowers were brand new. Their stitches and lace lines were pulled tight. Angus was viewing the situation with a keen eye and serious thought. At 1940 hours, our watch was called for 2000 hours. We were advised to don oilskins, for it was raining and 'breezing up'. By 2000 hours, the conventional bowline was being used. A loop is made in one end of a rope and is passed over a shoulder and under the opposite arm. The other end of the rope is made fast on deck. This is a preventative lifeline in case too much green water tumbles on deck and begins to push things around in the darkness. The captain, also, was 'oiled up' and on deck. He gave orders to get all hands on deck to take in the mainsail and jib. The topsails and staysail had been taken down before dark. In all probability, *Bluenose* was making twelve knots and all was safe on deck. Someone suggested they keep the mainsail up and try for record time. Someone, with more authority, was more concerned with keeping the mainsail in good shape for racing. The sail was furled.

The area of the mainsail was, approximately, 2300 sq. ft. The boom was 82 ft, and the gaff 45 ft. It is a lesson in seamanship the way the sail was furled that night. In gusty wind and choppy water, half a dozen men went out on the bowsprit to lower and secure the jib. Then they stood by to lower the mainsail. The throat and peak halyards were allowed to run free. The gaff came down in smart order. The mainboom was crutched and secured. Most of the sail was out over the starboard side, in the water. *Bluenose* had slowed down to about eight knots. The wheel was turned to port, which brought the bow pointing up into the wind. The heavy wet canvas tumbled aboard, where, in no time, it was rolled up on the boom and tied with special rope stops. This time, the helm was turned to starboard. The bow veered off and fixed on the course for Eastern Point buoy.

After a few strokes on the bilge pumps and a routine check, no leaks were reported. In spite of the last four hours of wind and choppy seas, all was well. Angus passed the wheel over to the watch and named the course. The watch repeated it. Angus ordered, "Pass the word to call me if the weather worsens or the fog shuts down." Then he disappeared to his cabin and his bunk for a few hours rest, secure in the knowledge that a sharp lookout and good wheelsman could keep things under control and safe. They had done it many times before, as part of the day's work.

The gusty 25 knot wind stayed with us until daylight, for an average speed of twelve knots. For the four hours between 1600 and 2000, prior to taking down the mainsail, it's safe to say *Bluenose* was doing 14 knots. Her coefficient and buoyancy value were unique in schooner design. The bow would split the crest of a head swell, then displace the water, making it roll out over and back under, to cause a lifting effect to the hull. During one race one of the crew, Kenneth Spidel, and I, spent about 20 minutes out on the end of the bowsprit, replacing a strained shackle.

Bluenose was doing about ten knots by the wind. Under the lee bow at water line the bow wave rolled out, down and inboard, making an air tunnel not less than 18 inches in diameter. There was a constant roaring sound which only restless sea-water can make. We took our time returning inboard. It was a fascinating sight to see 10,000 sq. ft of wind filled white canvas, the long black hull laying over to a twelve degree angle and pushing a huge bow wave of white foam. We had a full view of the entire vessel, from 18 feet beyond the stem. It was a sight to remember.

During the Gloucester trip, the men out on the bowsprit had a different situation, while furling the jib. When men are working on the bowsprit, the vessel is kept off before the wind. This is general seamanship practice. Out there, foot ropes and guy wires provide good protection. It is not unusual to have the bow settle down on the crest of a swell. Suddenly, you find yourself waist deep in the sea. If it is dark, you don't see the swell coming. Just as it starts to happen, you feel the bow settling down. This warns you to get your feet and legs, and, at least, one arm clenched to the foot ropes and wires. The other arm may be required to hold down the sail. Finally, the bow will raise and you are hard at work again, until the sail is secure.

Lunenburg fairway had been left 25 hours before, when *Bluenose* and *Thebaud* passed each other in Gloucester Harbour. They exchanged greetings, using fog horn sound signals. *Thebaud* was passing Ten Pound Island, outbound on tests. *Bluenose* was inbound.

The Gloucester berth was at Gorton and Pew Company, a large fish processing firm. They provided us with shed floor space and jetty side facilities. For the next four days, the crew earned their keep. The two engines, and all component parts, were put ashore. The vessel was hauled out. The 'A' frames for the propellers, shaft logs and bearings were also removed and put ashore. *Bluenose* was then undocked, ready to be trimmed with the iron ballast. Up to this point, the operation had gone smoothly. Bits and pieces had been taken apart and stored in a well organized manner.

Suddenly, there were strangers in our midst. They were armed with plumb-bobs and long poles. The poles were marked and graduated in feet and inches. They had come to check the water-line. It had been checked and found correct in the early series, as was required by the deed of gift specifications. But 18 years of rigging and ballasting to a trim will alter things. The hull was hogged and it was very unlikely the water-line markers would coincide, as in former days. Excess water-line length was not a problem for *Bluenose*. The forward draught could be reduced and the long raking stem would shorten the water-line. However, that would not be enough. The water-line length and the distribution of the inboard ballast must be properly co-ordinated. The master and several crew members were qualified to come up with a satisfactory formula.

Had the engines been left home in Lunenburg and the water-line fixed there, there would have not been the same problem. Sufficient ballast to compensate for engine weight could have been put on board.

The reading from the graduated poles and plumb-bobs showed that *Bluenose* had a maximum water-line. This decision played havoc with the moral of the crew, for the balance of the day. The water-line measurements were correct but the vessel was down by the head and out of trim. The crew were very unhappy. They were agreed about the water-line length, but not about the trim. The location and weight of the ballast control the trim, by which specified water-line length can be made to relate. Eventually, a compromise was made, but it was not entirely satisfactory. Time would prove the vessel was not in the best of trim. In addition, most of the ballast was onshore in the shed.

With each passing minute, the whole affair was becoming more of a worry to the crew. They had discovered that the old water-line markings were not in line anymore. The large head copper nails were about five inches too high amidships, when compared with fore and aft. Of course, this was not the fault of the Committee. It remained to be seen what would happen.

Imagine Ben Pine and Angus Walters meeting in an hotel lobby, that evening, and greeting each other with the natural question, "Well, how did things go today, Captain?" Anyone who has had the pleasure to meet fishing schooner captains, in a social way, would have no difficulty in picturing the conversation that followed!

The first race was off Boston, 9 October. It was more of a trial run for *Bluenose*. She was awkward to handle. There was a hidden fracture in the bowsprit, which developed into a clean break, soon after trimming the sheets for windward work. This caused the jib stays to come slack and let the bow fall to leeward rather than point up. The result was one race for *Gertrude L. Thebaud*. *Bluenose* requested time to make repairs.

We were grateful to Bethlehem and Pridgeon, of East Boston, for their ship repair facilities. In less than two days, a shiny new Douglas fir bowsprit held the jib stays secure. There was not time enough to apply paint. That would come later. The new jib would be free of black paint stains, for a while.

The few tons of ballast were squared away onboard. The second race, off Gloucester, was an easy win for *Bluenose*. She was lighter in ballast than she had ever been before, in a racing event. Naturally, this would be an advantage in a moderate wind.

It was not unusual to find half a dozen crewmen working late at night. They might be repairing a strained ringbolt, or a broken block, or a number of other things. In 18 years, the life expectancy of many parts of a Grand Bank fishing vessel grows less and less. During a race is not the best time to be confronted with worn out gear. Much time has to be devoted to repair or replacement.

After the delay, there sprang up a fresh 18 knot northwest wind, and the schooners made ready for the third race. Both crews were grateful for this. They longed for, and welcomed, the rattle of canvas and the crafty manoeuvering for the start. But it was not to be, for, luckily or unluckily, depending upon how you look at it, an accident happened just five minutes before the firing of the starting gun. *Bluenose's* geared wheel spindle broke. It fell out of the captain's hands and crashed to the deck. Sheets were trimmed by the wind, with the four lowers and topsails set. She was speeding along at not less than nine knots, and heading in the direction of 'Norman's Woe', a dry reef. Fortunately, *Thebaud* and other sailing craft were not in close range. It was a situation which would have been difficult to contend with in traffic or limited searoom. Angus, as usual, was quick to react. He ordered stand bys to all sheets. Then, by a process of sheeting in on certain sails and slacking away on others, *Bluenose* responded and came about on the other tack. A 'not under command' signal was soon acknowledged by a small coast guard patrol boat. It, in turn, notified the Committee boat and *Thebaud*. Then it returned to stand by, as moral support, until help arrived. An inbound fishing dragger came alongside and pushed *Bluenose* up the harbour, leaving her at the wharf.

Needless to say, this was very embarrassing. A beautiful racing day had been lost. Neither of the crews wanted the delay. Most of the men were committed to only a limited time away from their own regular fishing schooners. The consideration given by the crew of *Thebaud* was appreciated more than words could express.

The Edison steering mechanism, fitted on most Gloucester vessels, was very similar to the Lunenburg Foundry gear, but not closely enough to interchange parts. The problem was solved by the ingenuity of a skilled shipyard machinist. By noon, next day, the steering wheel was back in place, spinning and pushing the rudder from 'hard-a-port' to 'hard-a-starboard', just as it had been doing for the previous 18 years.

It was a relief to be back at the starting line, once more. Hopefully, this would see the completion of the third race. Spirits were somewhat dampened. There was almost an obsession with the fear that another accident would happen. The sky was overcast and a fresh south wind prevailed throughout the day. The water soaked planks and timbers, below the waterline, provided more effective ballast than the few pieces of iron and beach rocks in the hold. *Bluenose* was fast, sometimes rolling out a high windward side. At one point, from marker buoy to marker buoy, she was doing twelve knots under slightly eased sheets. Also, it is likely *Thebaud* reached close to her maximum speed. When two schooners sail closely and under the same conditions for five hours, and stay within one mile apart, there is no time for mistakes or broken gear. *Bluenose* crossed the finish line six and one half minutes ahead of *Thebaud*, and was the winner of the third race.

The deck head of a fishing schooner forecastle is painted a bright gloss white. (The deck head is the underside of the main deck.) It is painted white in order to reflect light and to brighten a large closed in area which is devoid of a port light, or glass window of any sort. The Oregon pine foremast is stepped down through the deck to the keel. It is of natural colour and shines from many coats of varnish.

The foremast is large. The shiny white and varnished surfaces form an interesting contrast, where they meet. Soon after the first table sitting for supper, that evening, it was discovered that the pleasant contrast of white and varnish was separated by a dark brown ring space, of about three inches in width. It was an example of the strain to which the vessel had been put while racing. The wind pressure on the sails created stress which came down through the rigging and back stays which, in turn, caused the deck to be raised. It had settled back to a more normal position, by breakfast, next morning.

Preparations were made for an early start for the 25 mile run to Boston, where the fourth race was to be held. The fresh southerly wind, which had done so much for us the day before, had moderated during the night. Instead, a dense fog had settled in. It blanketed the coast all the way from Cape Cod to Maine. The easterly wind was very gentle. *C.G.S. Arras* accompanied *Bluenose* to Boston. She was her official escort.

Onboard, were several Gloucester citizens who had come along to enjoy the trip aboard a racing schooner. They would not remain in Boston but take the commuter train back to Gloucester. It's a straight run of 15 miles from Cape Ann to Graves Light. From there to the Boston water-front is a further nine miles through an irregular, but well buoyed, channel. The light breeze and fog caused anxiety to the passengers. They feared they would miss their connection with the commuter train, but they were saved by the *C.G.S. Arras* which came alongside and towed *Bluenose* for the last five miles.

The Committee decided that the following day would be a 'lay day'. This time, it was *Thebaud* who was asking for the delay. She had bumped a rock while sailing from Gloucester Harbour. She was hauled out, examined and repaired.

Boston is a very nice city in which to spend a day ashore.

It, also, had its drawbacks for the crew. They had amateur status, as far as wages were concerned. Window shopping, in downtown Boston, is a dangerous occupation. Pedestrians move quickly along the sidewalks. We had to keep our eyes open and be on the move, too.

The weather continued to be dull with light winds, and we were grateful to *Thebaud* for the day ashore. All hands found something interesting or amusing. It was good, because next day dawned with a fresh WNW wind.

Gertrude L. Thebaud was off Cape Nahant, making the same smart manoeuvering tactics, as always. Jockeying for position was becoming a routine. Gusty 18 to 20 knot winds made things unpredictable. The large schooners were moving quickly. Angus took a walk forward to midships and cautioned the crew to be ready for anything. "For," said he, "you can never tell what that fellow is up to." He gave further instructions and ended with the warning, "Just don't foul things up." This was taken as an order.

It was not unusual, before starting time, for a captain to decide to sail his vessel close under the stern of the other and to call out some humourous remark, as a friendly gesture. Needless to say, the remark was in no way related to international schooner racing.

Crossing over the starting line with five to nine schooners could be exciting. In the elimination contests, sometimes the vessels would be so close that the mainsail and mainboom of a boat could well be inboard and directly over the deck of a rival vessel. However, with only two schooners, it was more practical to stay a resonable distance apart. This would avoid luffing and the wasting of time. It was that way in the race off Nahant.

On the reach down the first leg, the two vessels were close to each other until it came to windward work. Here, *Bluenose* opened up a good lead. Suddenly, Angus decided to tack and cover *Thebaud*. When *Bluenose* was given too much wheel, she would come around so quickly it would be hard to trim the sheets in time. Undoubtedly, this had something to do with the staysail fouling in the gate of the mainmast head. The sail ripped from head to foot. The tear was, at least, 40 feet long. In a loud and clear voice, Angus yelled, "It's no good up there, that way. Get it down."

Down it came, in record time, but Kenny, the rigger, had his sail-bag ready. The bag was kept under the saddle of the mainmast. It contained a couple of iron splicing fids, a ball of sail twine, a junk of bee's wax, a lump of hard tallow, four sewing palms, a monkey wrench, a carpenter's hammer which had a very short handle, a few eyelets, grummet rings and about a dozen sail-needles threaded with waxed sail twine. Because the rigger had his sail-bag in order, quickly the rip was mended. Within ten minutes of the sail falling on the deck, the tear was herring-bone stitched from top to bottom and ready to be hoisted. In the meantime, a smaller and dirty spare was pulled up from the hold and hoisted. It was a poor looking sail and did not fit. But it was not up there for long. When the order came 'hard a-lee', the vessel tacked and the regular staysail went up again. Officials onboard the Committee boat were jotting down notes. Was there going to be a protest? Certainly, there would be, if *Bluenose* was carrying three staysails contrary to the rules.

It was settled, later that night, when the staysail was taken onshore and spread out on the floor of the fish pier Exchange Room. There was no argument when the inspectors saw approximately 1400 herringbone stitches. There were three stitches to the inch. We were thankful to Kenny and the traditional sail-bag.

About half-way around the course, the weather conditions became overcast, with reduced visibility and light rain squalls. Up to this point, *Bluenose* had won two races and *Thebaud* one. *Bluenose* was now in the lead, with less than three miles to the finish line. It looked as if the trying ordeal would soon be over. However, this was not to be. Suddenly, the foretopmast stay came loose with a loud snap. The topmast bent like an archer's bow. The man aloft did some gymnastic feats amongst the flapping canvas and wires. Angus saw it happen and, as usual, was quick to respond. He brought *Bluenose* up in the wind and about. This would put the strain on the opposite stay and prevent the topmast from breaking. The balloon and foretopsail were lowered and furled. The accident happened when a special knot in the end of the hemp lanyard was pulled through the hole in a worn lignumvitae deadeye, causing the backstay to go adrift. Angus ordered us to secure the stay, so that we could come about on a course to the finish line, without the danger of breaking the topmast. While this was being attended to, *Thebaud* sailed past. Captain Cecil Moulton was at the wheel. He had replaced Captain Pine for this race. Relatively speaking, *Thebaud* was a new vessel and had not yet reached the point when fair wear and tear becomes a problem.

Now the score was even, at two races each. The next race would be off Gloucester and would decide the championship.

It is seven miles from 'the Graves' to Boston Harbour. The northwest wind made it a dead beat. Soon after crossing the line, each vessel had taken on some passengers. They were from some of the small pleasure craft, and were anxious to have the thrill of sailing into Boston onboard a racing schooner. Balloon, staysail and topsails were furled for the day. We would beat in under four lowers.

The passengers were treated to a thrilling experience as we beat up Boston Harbour. The event developed into a competitive affair and became very exciting in the narrow channel. Both captains had turned the wheel over to a crew member and, no doubt, were below deck enjoying a 'coffee', possibly an Irish coffee. I remember, quite well, who was at the wheel of *Bluenose*, and how close both schooners were. In fact, channel buoy #5 was all that separated the two. *Bluenose* rounded the buoy to get weather position and take the lead. Fortunately, the competition was short lived.

The schooners became the guests of a harbour tugboat and were pushed alongside the Boston Fish Pier. The citizens of Boston were splendid hosts.

Our crew worked late that night. The worn deadeye was replaced and the staysail put ashore in the sail loft for repairs. Reward for our labour was sweetened with a generous supply of liquid refreshment and tobacco. These were given with the compliments of various wholesale business houses.

Up to this point, the series had been extremely wearisome and time consuming, especially for the crew. Suddenly, there was a great change in the general attitude. It was possible for *Gertrude L. Thebaud* to win the series and The

58

Halifax Herald Trophy, thus making the United States custodian of all three trophies, the Halifax Herald Trophy, the 100 Guineas Cup and the Sir Thomas Lipton Cup. Such a possibility put *Bluenose* in a precarious position, much more so than in any past series. For all were well aware of *Bluenose*'s weather beaten condition, caused by 18 years of rugged life on the North Atlantic Ocean, of her having been laden with heavy loads of salt cod fish, and of being hogged. In this condition, she must face what would probably be the one and final opportunity to defend the honoured title, 'Queen of the North Atlantic Fishing Schooners', a title which paid handsome tribute to naval architecture, shipbuilding and seamanship.

The odds could be rated even, judging by the recent performance of the two vessels. In a way, both crews realized this event would be making history.

On the morning, 26 October, the weather conditions were cloudy, with cool west winds averaging 15 to 18 knots. The visibility was good, off the Massachusetts coast.

Both vessels were manoeuvering about the Cape Ann starting line, long before start time. Finally, the count down commenced. Under full sail, both schooners headed toward the line. Seconds after the gun, Captain Ben Pine had *Thebaud* across it. Captain Walters positioned *Bluenose* close behind, but to windward. Soon after, he sailed her out in the lead and continued a gradual increase on every leg of the course. *Thebaud* was close behind. Only three minutes separated them at any one time. Therefore, *Bluenose* could not afford to make a mistake or have a mishap. The reader should try to visualize the magnitude of those schooners with their lofty rig and volume of sail. Imagine that you are an observer on the deck of one and watching the other only yards astern, with lee rail awash and travelling at the rate of twelve knots. It is a beautiful picture and an awesome sight, demanding respect.

The wind, when properly harnessed, provides that mysterious power for propelling sail-driven vessels. It becomes their constant and challenging companion.

When the two schooners were closing in on the finish line, there was an awareness of something unusual in the bahaviour of the wind, as though it understood what was happening at the moment would, in future, be remembered as the end of an era. It seemed as if it were saying,

"This is your most glorious hour. Who knows better than I that my special demonstration of force drives you happily and honourably to fame?"

The old schooner responded in courtesy fashion, occasionally, by dipping her lee rail awash, as proudly she sailed towards the finish line.

A short tack was required to fetch and cross the line. When *Bluenose* came about, the main topmast staysail halyard block broke, in yield to the stress. This caused the halyard to jam, which prevented the staysail from being properly set for the port tack. Otherwise it was not serious. The sail was almost in normal position. Pulling hard on her sheets, *Bluenose* crossed the finish line two minutes and fifty seconds ahead of *Thebaud* and, officially, was declared the winner of the 1938 series.

In referring to the end of an era, it should be remembered that the emphasis goes far beyond that schooner race event. Except for some few isolated places and small coastal craft, it was the end for large commercial sailing vessels, all over the world. Perhaps it was destined that those two beautiful, fast and able schooners should write 'finis' in such a colourful manner.

The series completed, *Bluenose* loaded her engines, component parts and the controversial ballast. She sailed home to Lunenburg.

There, she was greeted by a modest number of townsfolk, friends and relatives of the crew. Nothing could be more sincere than the handshakes and complimentary remarks, for these were people who understood the amount of effort and unfailing courage involved in the defence of the Trophy and the honour connected with it.

The schooner *Bluenose* brought fame to Canada and fame for industrial skill and seamanship. It is not too late to erect a memorial in her honour.

Appendix "A"

Description of a 'Grand Banker'.

The term 'Grand Banker' was commonly used along the Atlantic New England States, Canadian Maritime Provinces and Newfoundland until 1930.

The description of a Grand Banker is as follows:

(a) A wood construction fore and aft rigged two masted sailing schooner

(b) Its dimensions ranged in size from
110'0A 23'B 10' depth up to
145'0A 27'B 15.6' depth

(c) It was employed in the salt cod fishery. It would go out on the fishing banks for cod. The fish were split and salted in bulk, down the hold, until the schooner was full. Then the vessel would return to home port and discharge the cargo of fish for sun drying, before marketing.

(d) The fish were caught by the baited hook and line trawl method. The schooner was brought to anchor and the dories were dropped off to set out the trawl lines, from which they would return 'underrun'. Later, the dorymen would inspect the trawls, remove the fish, rebait, return to the schooner and bring the fish onboard where it was split, washed and salted down.

(e) Some vessels would carry six dories, some eight, and

some ten, depending on the size and carrying capacity of the schooner. There were two men to a dory.

The trawl lines, averaging 240 yards in length, were set out in fan fashion off each side of the schooner. Thus, when the schooner chose a spot and came to anchor, she would occupy a circle area with a radius of, at least, one mile.

(f) Common sense specifications called for a strong, seaworthy schooner, capable of carrying a large catch and having reasonable manoeuvering and sailing qualities.

Appendix B

Record of Seamen Shipped at the Port of Lunenburg, N.S., 29 September 1938

The following men signed on as crew of the Schooner *Bluenose*, 79 tons, registered at Lunenburg, N.S., for a term of six months, beginning 29/9/38, terminating in Canada. Captain's name Angus J. Walters.

Seaman's Name	Age	Birth place	Name of Seaman's last ship	Capacity	Wages
Geo. A. Myra	32	Lunenburg	*Bluenose*	Sailor	22.00
Borden Andersen	22	Lunenburg	*Bluenose*	Sailor	22.00
Irving Corkum	40	Middle LaHave	*Gloria May*	Sailor	22.00
Harold Corkum	52	Middle LaHave	*Ruby May*	Sailor	22.00
Samuel Shaw	70	Dartmouth	*Elizabeth Noonen*	Sailor	22.00
Claude Darrach	35	Herring Cove	*Researcher*	Sailor	22.00
Clyde Eisnor	27	River Port	*Isebel Spindler*	Sailor	22.00
Lloyd Heisler	33	Indian Point	*Gerlrude Jean*	Sailor	22.00
John Pardy	39	Lunenburg	*Bluenose*	Sailor	22.00
Herbert Hardiman	22	Bellorman Nfld.	*Howard Donald*	Sailor	22.00
Thomas Black	25	Lunenburg	*Bluenose*	Sailor	22.00
Arthur Corkum	26	Lunenburg	First ship	Sailor	22.00

Name	Age	Place	Ship	Role	
Douglas Pyke	32	Lunenburg	*Bluenose*	Sailor	22.00
Henry Banfield	31	Bay Largent Nfld.	*Harry Admans*	Sailor	22.00
Lawrence Hoover	30	Boston	*Alta C.*	Sailor	22.00
J. Fracie Williams	30	Halifax	*Nicopsie*	Passenger	00.25
Doris Day	38	American Fall River Conn.	*Melbarlin*	Passenger	00.25
Edward Briggs	32	American	*Maid of Bara*	Passenger	00.25
Borden McCellen	20	Lunenburg	First ship	Passenger	00.25
Stewart Walters	22	Lunenburg	*Bluenose*	Passenger	00.25
Marion Falkenham	21	Lunenburg	First ship	Passenger	00.25
Mrs. W. Lawrence Sweeney	29	Yarmouth	*Marie Stewart*	Passenger	00.25
Kenneth Spidel	62	Lunenburg	*Andrava*	Sailor	22.00
Philip Poole	28	Newfoundland	*Robert & Douglas*	Sailor	22.00
Cyril Hiltz	22	Martin's Point	*Bluenose*	Sailor	22.00
Adam Knickle	82	Lunenburg	*Bluenose*	Sailor	22.00
Lawrence Allen	40	Lunenburg	*Bluenose*	Mate	70.00
Fred Rhodenizer	37	Lunenburg	*Bluenose*	Sailor	22.00
Horace Miller	28	Lunenburg	*Clarence Morrow*	Sailor	22.00
James E. Whynot	50	Stone Hurst	*Bluenose*	Cook	22.00
G.C. Burgoyne	47	Mahone Bay	*M/S Muir*	Sailor	22.00
*Capt. Moyle Crouse		Lunenburg	*Haligonian*	Sailor	22.00
*Paul Crouse		Lunenburg	*Haligonian*	Sailor	

*Joined ship in Gloucester

Appendix C

THE HALIFAX HERALD'S

(International)

F I S H E R M E N ' S   T R O P H Y

Conditions of Deed of Gift.

To all Men

G R E E T I N G S

Be it known that William H. Dennis, representing the proprietors of *The Halifax Herald* and *The Evening Mail* newspapers, published in the City of Halifax, in the Province of Nova Scotia, Canada, recognizing the great importance and value of the deep sea fishing industry to the inhabitants of this Province of Nova Scotia, and realizing the necessity of the best possible type of craft being employed in the pursuit of the industry and believing that this can best be obtained by engendering a spirit of friendly competition among the fishermen of this Province and also with the fishermen engaged in similar methods of fishing in the other Maritime Provinces of Canada, the Dominion of Newfoundland and the United States of America, has donated and placed under the control of Trustees to be named herein, a TROPHY, of which a photograph and description thereof shall be attached hereto,

65

to be known as:

THE HALIFAX HERALD
NORTH ATLANTIC FISHERMEN'S
INTERNATIONAL TROPHY

to be sailed for annually under the Rules and Conditions which follow, which may be added to, taken from or modified from time to time to meet changing conditions of the Industry by the Trustees herein appointed or their successors. The said Rules or any modification thereof being always drawn in such manner as to safeguard and continue the intention of the Donors of the Trophy, which is the development of the most practical and serviceable type of fishing schooner combined with the best sailing qualities, without sacrificing utility. For the purpose of maintaining this principle the Trustees are empowered to disqualify from all or any competition any vessel which in their opinion is of such a type or dimensions as would contravene the intention of the Donors and such decisions of the Trustees shall be final: the Trustees shall, however, do nothing which will change the spirit of the intention of the Donors, that the competition shall be confined to vessels and crews engaged in practical commercial fishing.

The Trustees in whom the control of the Trophy is vested are The Honourable The Premier of Nova Scotia, His Worship The Mayor of Halifax, Messrs. H.R. Silver, H.G. DeWolf, R.A. Corbett, H.G. Lawrence, W.J. Roue, F.W. Baldwin, Capt. V.C. Johnson, being Members of the Original Committee; any vacancies to be filled by a majority vote of the remaining Trustees, who, in conference with the representatives of the Gloucester Committee in charge of the races held in the year Nineteen Hundred and Twenty, have drawn the following Rules and Regulations, which shall govern all future races until and unless good and sufficient reason arises for their modification in such manner as the Trustees may consider advisable.

1. This Trophy is being presented by the proprietors of *The Halifax Herald* and *The Evening Mail*, as a perpetual International Championship Trophy, to be raced for annually.

2. All Races for this Trophy shall be under the control and management of an International Committee of Five,

which shall be elected for each series of races; the Trustees will nominate the two members of the Committee to represent Nova Scotia, and the Governor of the Commonwealth of Massachusetts, in conjunction with the local United States Committee handling the Race, shall name the two members of the Committee to represent the United States. The Chairman of this Committee shall be named by the two members of the Committee representing the country in which the Race is to be held.

3. The Race shall be sailed in the year 1921 off the Harbour of Halifax, Nova Scotia, and alternately thereafter off Gloucester (or a course in Massachusetts Bay to be mutually agreed upon by the International Committee in charge of the Race) and off Halifax, Nova Scotia. The dates on which the Races are to be sailed shall be decided by the International Committee, but shall be fixed so as not to unduly interfere with the business in which the craft are engaged.

4. The only vessels which can compete for the Trophy shall be bona fide fishing vessels, which have been engaged in commercial deep sea fishing for at least one season previous to the Race. A fishing season for the purpose of these Rules is considered as extending from the month of April to September, and any vessel competing must have actually sailed from her last port of departure for the Fishing Banks not later than April thirtieth in any year and have remained on the fishing grounds in all weather as customary, until the month of September, excepting necessary returns to port for landing cargo and refitting. Fishing Banks shall mean all off-shore Banks, such as George's, Western, Grand, etc., and vessels engaged in shore fishing and making port in bad weather shall not be eligible.

5. The Captain and Crew of each competing vessel shall be bona fide fishermen, actively engaged in deep sea fishing, and the number of the crew shall be fixed by the International Committee. A list of the crew of each vessel and substitutes therefor shall be forwarded to the International Committee one week before the Series takes place, and each vessel competing shall be furnished with a copy of the Crew List of the opposing vessel or vessels.

6. All competing vessels shall be propelled by sails only

and must comply with the following measurements and conditions:

(a) **Overall Length,** Not to exceed one hundred and forty-five (145) feet, from outside of stem to outside of taffrail.

(b) **Water Line Length,** in racing trim, not to exceed one hundred and twelve (112) feet from outside of stem at point of submersion to point of submersion at the stern.

(c) **Draught of Vessel** in racing trim shall not exceed sixteen (16) feet from the lowest point of the keel to the racing water line, measured vertically.

(d) No **Outside Ballast** shall be used.

(e) **Inside Ballast** shall consist of any material of a not greater specific gravity than iron.

(f) **Competing Vessels** shall race with the same spars, including booms and gaffs (which must all be solid), as are used in fishing.

(g) **Competing Vessels** must be of the usual type, both in form and construction, sail plan and rigging, as customary in the fishing industry, and any radical departure therefrom may be regarded as a freak and eliminated.

7. (a) **The Sails** used in racing shall be made of the ordinary commercial duck of the same weight and texture as generally used in this class of vessel and shall have been used at least one season in fishing.

(b) **Sails to be Used** are Mainsail, Foresail, two jibs, (including Jumbo), Jib Topsail, Fore and Main Gaff Topsails and fisherman's Staysail.

(c) **The Total Sail Area,** not including fisherman's Staysail, to be no greater than Eighty Percent (80%) of the square of the water line length, in racing trim, as expressed in square feet. This stipulation not to apply to vessels built previous to the 1920 Races, but such existing vessels shall not increase their sail area to exceed 80% of the square of the water line if it does not already do so.

(d) **The Combined Area** of the Mainsail and Main Gaff Topsail shall not be more than Fifty Percent (50%) of the maximum total sail area, as provided in the preceding subsection "c".

8. The area of the sails shall be calculated as follows:

Mainsail. By the universal rule for mainsails, with the exception that the "B" of the formulae shall be measured from the after-side of the mainmast to the outer clew iron hole.
Main Gaff Topsail. Universal rule.
Foresail and Fore Gaff Topsail. By the universal rule for actual measurement of the sails used and not a percentage of space between the masts.
Head Sails. Universal rule for Head Sails.

If more than one Staysail or Jibtopsail are on the vessel they must be of the same area and only one can be set at a time.

9. **No Ballast** shall be taken on or put off the competing vessels during the Series and no ballast shall be shifted after the Fifteen Minute Preparatory Gun is fired before each Race.

10. **The International Committee** shall have power to arrange all details of the Races in accordance with the Deed of Gift and shall appoint such Sub-Committees as may be necessary to properly carry them out.

11. **The Sailing Committee** shall be a sub-committee, appointed by the International Committee, and shall be an independent body having no financial interest in the competing vessels. They will lay out the courses for each Series, decide the Course to be sailed for each Race, make the necessary sailing regulations and have them carried out.

12. **The Courses** laid down by the sailing committee shall not be less than thirty-five or more than forty nautical miles in length and be so arranged as to provide windward and leeward work. The time limit of each Race shall be nine hours. There shall be no handicap or time allowance, each vessel shall be on its merits.

13. **The Trophy** shall be awarded to and remain in the possession for one year of the Vessel winning Two out of Three **Races** over Courses as laid down by the sailing committee each year, and a responsible person or corporation representing the Owners of the winning vessel shall give to the Trustees of the Trophy an official receipt therefor, together with a Bond for $500.00, obligating them to return the Trophy to the Trustees

previous to the next Race to replace the Trophy if it becomes lost or destroyed through accident or otherwise; and to return same to the Trustees if it has not been raced for during a period of five years.

14. **The Total Cash Prizes** awarded in connection with this Race in any one year shall not exceed the sum of Five Thousand Dollars ($5,000) for each Series and the distribution of the money shall be decided by the International Committee. The money for these prizes to be provided by the Committee representing the country in which the Race is held.

If for any reason there should be no International Competition for this Trophy for any period of five consecutive years it shall be within the power of the Trustees to make such use of the Trophy as they may consider advisable in connection with the development of the Fishing Industry in the Province of Nova Scotia.

In Witness Whereof we have hereunto set our hands and affixed our seals this 23rd day of March, in the year of our Lord One Thousand Nine Hundred and Twenty-One A.D.

In the presence of

(sgd.) W.H. DENNIS
for the Proprietors of *The Halifax Herald*
and *The Evening Mail*

(sgd.) H.R. SILVER
For the Trustees

70

Appendix D

During the conclusive stages of the manuscript the peak of the yacht racing season off Block Island R.I., USA arrived, bringing once again the century old challenge and competition for the famous 'America Cup'. (The trophy formerly known as the 100 Guinea Cup and won by the U.S. yacht *America* in a race round the Isle of White, 1851).

This year the entries are "British — *Victory 83*", "Canadian — *Canada I*", "France — *France III*", "Australia — *Australia II*", "Italian — *Azzura*", and of course the United States defender — *Liberty*. Obviously these boats are up to date with the latest and best of sails, rigging and technical mechanism. However, in addition *Australia II*'s design included a simple but entirely new gimmick, a winged-keel, which of course caused the committee some concern. However, after timely and careful consideration it was decided *Australia II*'s entry be accepted and she compete on the same basis as all other entries.

During the series of elimination races it was soon proven *Australia II* was a fast boat and manouvered well. Indeed at the present time little is known of the theory and basics of the gimmick but winged-keel or not, *Australia II* under command of a skilled and experienced skipper and crew, for the first time in 133 years out sailed and beat the U.S. defender and took the America Cup to Australia.

Starting out as the 100 Guinea Cup, now the America Cup, generated much enthusiasm and research in design and popularity for 133 years. Actually the development of sail has been an international study since the Egyptian boat of 6000 B.C. confirming man's traditional fascination for the sea.

Glossary

Banks — Grand, George's, Sable Island, Western

Belaying Pin — wooden or iron pin to secure running rope

Carling — timber used in construction of the hull

Coefficient — part of a formula used to determine the dead weight of a ship, ranging from .4 to .8

Deadeye — lignumvitae fair leads through which the lanyards pass

Downhauls — ropes for pulling down the outer jibs and other sails

Eyebolts — fixed bolts to which various types of tackle are attached

Grand Bank — the large area of shallow depth terrain east of Newfoundland. At one point, the Virgin Rocks are awash. The entire area is noted for its abundance of cod fish.

Halyard — rope for raising or lowering sails

Highliner — having a record quantity of fish

Hogged — when the bow and stern ends of a schooner commence to droop

Jibe — to bring the sails over from port side to starboard side, or vice versa, when running before the wind

Jury-rig — a rig contrived from whatever masts, sails and rigging are left after having been ravaged by a heavy gale

Knockabout — fore and aft rigged schooner without a bowsprit

Luff — to cause a sailing vessel to point up close to the wind

Sea State — a sailor's word. The meaning is obvious.

Shackles — connecting link with a screw pin

Shaft Log — water tight facility encasing the propeller shaft

Sheer Poles — steel bar attached to the mast head shrouds, spacing the deadeyes and lanyards

Sheets — the ropes and blocks that control the trimming in and the slacking out of the booms and sails

Shrouds — set of ropes forming part of standing rigging and supporting mast or topmast

Stays — wire rope supporting mast or spar

Wheelsman — a helmsman

Schooners that competed in trials and series events 1920-1938
International Fishermans' Schooner Race
For The Halifax Herald Trophy

Schooner	Master	Remarks
Delewana	T. Himmelman	First winner & defender 1920
Gilbert Walters	A. Walters	second place in first race
Alcala	R. Knickle	third place in first race
Bernice Zinck	D. Zinck	conventional design
Mona Marie	L. Ritchey	conventional design
Ruby L. Pentz	C. Lohnes	conventional design Capt. lost at sea returning home after race 1920
Independence	A. Himmelman	conventional design
Democracy	Wm. Deal	conventional design
Freda Himmelman	A. Himmelman	conventional design
Esperanto (U.S.)	M. Welch	winner of the The Trophy Oct. 1920 lost at sea 1921
Elizabeth Howard (U.S.)	B. Pine	conventional design
L.A. Dunton (U.S.)	Hogan	U.S. defender 1921, replacing Esperanto and lost trophy to Bluenose
Elsie (U.S.)	M. Welch	
Bluenose	A. Walters	

J. Duffy	Spindler	conventional design
Ada Corkum	Corkum	conventional design
Donald Cook	Cook	conventional design
Canadia	J. Conrad	Built in Shelburne
		a large fast schooner
Henry Ford (U.S.)	C. Morrissey	very good in light wind
Yankee (U.S.)		small and pretty
		not a good contender
Mahaska	P. Mack	beautiful schooner. not so fast
Margaret K. Smith	Demone	
Columbia (U.S.)	Pine, Wharton	close match for *Bluenose* in
		moderate winds
Haligonian	M. Crouse	lost at sea with all hands
		Aug. 24, 1927
Gertrude L. Thebaud (U.S.)	Pine	fast and pretty lines
		had trouble in heavy wind
Mayflower (U.S.)	Larkin	disqualified because of
		yacht-like design
Mayotte	Himmelman	lost at sea — never raced
Puritan (U.S.)	Jeff Thomas	lost at sea 4 months after launching
Keino	Himmelman	lost at sea all hands — never raced

Bluenose wrecked Caribeen Reef, Jan. 1946
Columbia lost off Sable Island, Aug. 24, 1927
Gertrude L. Thebaud wrecked La Quira Venz, Feb. 1948
Esperanto lost on Sable Island, May 30, 1921

The Author

Claude Darrach was born at Herring Cove, Nova Scotia. He is the son of a fishing schooner captain and believes the parental blood stream and local environment gave him no alternative but to a seafaring life and to grow up in an atmosphere of courage, skill, and truth which is not to be underestimated or forgotten. The reward is confidence and the essential basic to a grateful future.

A few years in the dory schooner on the banks, then he was employed for 12 years with the Biological Board, Fish Migration, on water temperature, off shore fishing banks. For six years, 1940-1946, he saw active service with the RCNR during world war two. Then he was with naval auxiliary vessels (mate and master) oceanographic research. He has had a life of uncertainty and struggle but always there has been a ray of hope on the horizon.

Now he is supposedly retired after several seasons as master M/V Haligonian III Charter Tours. He and his wife Eva live in Herring Cove where their roots are deepest and his fondest memories are of the men and schooners he knew so well.